MW01672667

# Called to Ecumenism

## A Sense of Vocation at Luther College

Ruth R. Kath

*With contributions from*

Marilyn Roverud, Wilfred Bunge,

Bishop April Ulring Larson,

Archbishop Jerome Hanus, O.S.B.,

Mark Muggli and Carol Gilbertson, Theodor Dieter,

Fr. Gary Krapfl

Lutheran University Press

Minnneapolis, Minnesota

**Called to Ecumenism**

A Sense of Vocation at Luther College

Ruth R. Kath,

*With contributions from* Marilyn Roverud, Wilfred Bunge, Bishop April Ulring Larson, Archbishop Jerome Hanus, O.S.B., Mark Muggli and Carol Gilbertson, Theodor Dieter, Fr. Gary Krapfi



Cover photo: "Walk to Church," Luther College 2004, Ruth R Kath
Back cover photo: Chip Peterson

Library of Congress Cataloging-in-Publication data

Kath, Ruth R.., 1948-

Called to ecumenism : a sense of vocation at Luther College / Ruth R. Kath, editor

p. cm.

ISBN - 13: 1-978-932688-13-9 (pbk.)

ISBN - 10: 1-932688-13-7

1. Luther College (Decorah, Iowa)—Religion. 2. Ecumenical movement—Iowa—Decorah—History. I. Kath, Ruth R., 1948-

BR561.L88C35 2006

230.07'3417732—dc22

2006044734

www.lutheranUpress.org

Lutheran University Press, PO Box 390759, Minnneapolis, Minnesota

Manufactured in the United States of America

For my father, Randolph B. Robert,

the first ecumenist in my life

# Table of Contents

# Preface

One of the most impressive aspects of Luther College has long been its faithfulness to its Lutheran roots that includes an invitation to people of other faith traditions to join the community. The way the Luther community welcomes its neighbors to join the conversation about faith and learning has intrigued me since my arrival over 25 years ago. A sabbatical leave in the fall of 2003 allowed me to chronicle this remarkable development of the longstanding call to ecumenism that has characterized Luther College since the early 1960s, a century after its founding as a college of the church.

Important to the telling of the Luther story are the voices of ecumenists who have helped to shape the vision of inclusion for the campus and for the town of Decorah in which it is situated. Records of their pioneering ecumenical work include the unpublished manuscript by Fr. Emeric Lawrence, O.S.B., now housed in the archives of St. John's Abbey in Collegeville, Minnesota, as well as other Emeric papers in the archives of Luther College in Decorah, Iowa. The papers of former Luther College presidents Dr. E.D. Farwell and Dr. H. George Anderson, both located in the Luther archives, also offered much valuable information.

Many others have joined their voices to help continue telling the story. Their reflections on the special ecumenical calling of this small liberal arts college of the church were offered in community public forums and featured in the college journal *Agora* at the college in recent years; they are reproduced here by kind permission of the *Agora* editor. Other reflections found their way to paper only because I asked the author about his or her ecumenical life. Among the most touching voices are those of the students who opened themselves to ecumenical formation, and now help to continue the story of ecumenism in this special place.

I am grateful to Bro. David Klingemann, O.S. B., archivist of St. John's Abbey and University, and to Rachel Vagts, archivist of Luther College, for their assistance with the papers mentioned above, as well as to Connie Barclay, Vocation Administrative Assistant. For their invaluable support of this project, I thank President Richard Torgerson, Dean William Craft, professor emeritus Wilfred Bunge, Professor Mark Muggli, and the Steering Committee of the Sense of Vocation program at Luther College, funded by a generous gift to the college from the Lilly Endowment, Inc. under its program for the Theological Exploration of Vocation. The careful work of editor Laura Callen and the encouragement of Leonard Flachman, Lutheran University Press, have helped to give the book its final shape. Finally, thank you to colleagues, past and present, in Decorah, Dubuque, Collegeville, Wittenberg, Strasbourg, and Rome for helping many generations of faithful students to learn the blessings, as well as the costs, of dedication to an ecumenical life.

# Introduction

**That they all may be one...**
John 17:21

In 2001, Luther College received a very generous $2 million grant from the Lilly Endowment, Inc., through the Fund for Theological Exploration of Vocation. This grant was used to establish the "Sense of Vocation" program at Luther College. Long before that, we had been thinking a great deal about vocation, for the students, faculty, and staff of this college of the Church. Questions of vocation are central to the college's Mission Statement, are included in the recent Strategic Plan and are basic to the Student Academic Goals for Achievement. Vocation has a long history at Luther College.

When we ask the vocation question, *What am I meant to do with my life?* we nearly always focus on individuals and their place within the larger communities in which they will live and function. The "Sense of Vocation" program has given me the opportunity to work on a project I had long wanted to undertake: the documentation of the unusual ecumenical cooperation between Lutherans and Roman Catholics that has characterized Luther College and the community of Decorah since the early 1960s. The focus of my research has been the college's call to ecumenism experienced in these years: the call to know the college's strong Lutheran roots, but also to welcome other religious traditions that enrich its life as a community of faith; in short, the special sense of Vocation that Luther College has long experienced.

This opportunity included research into archival materials, correspondence with former members of the Luther College faculty, both in Decorah and away, and conferences with others about their personal recollections and the experience. This book is the product. The project has been not only a unique contribution to the history of Luther College, but also valuable preparation for the ecumenical January Term study course with our Roman Catholic sister institution Loras College. The course in Rome and Wittenberg has now become a standard offering at the college.

The Luther College Archives holdings permitted close reading of the papers left by former college presidents Farwell and Anderson. Both of these men made major contributions to the development of ecumenism on the Luther campus and in the surrounding community. The archives at St. John's University and Abbey yielded important finds, including a full-length unpublished manuscript, "The Lutheran Journals of a Catholic Monk" one of many writings produced by Fr. Emeric Lawrence, O.S.B. during his years in Decorah. Conversations with others connected with the college have yielded the special written reflections in this book. These include essays by an emeritus faculty member about being the first Luther instructor to participate in a faculty exchange with St. John's; an essay by a member of the Luther Board of Regents on childhood memories of playing with a little Catholic neighbor girl; and a faculty couple on their ecumenical marriage and the celebration marking the 1999 signing of the *Joint Declaration on the Doctrine of Justification.*

E.D. Farwell pioneered ecumenical cooperation at Luther in 1963 by inviting the Roman Catholic archbishop of Dubuque to present a public lecture in the Valders Hall of Science. The archbishop's visit fostered warm ecumenical relations and a sense of shared Christian mission. Later that decade that attitude allowed the establishment of a one-to-one exchange of Religion faculty members between Luther and St. John's University in Collegeville, Minnesota.[1] The remarkable cooperative venture continued for eight years (1967–1975). During that time, one young Luther faculty member in Religion after another spent a year at St. John's. At Luther the exchange was inhabited by one monk, the inimitable Fr. Emeric Lawrence, O.S.B., for six of the eight years. Emeric loved Decorah, and quickly acquired the respect and love of the Luther community.

H. George Anderson assumed the presidency of Luther College in 1981, and, over the fourteen years of his tenure, brought ecumenism in

Decorah and in the rest of the country and world to new heights. For many years, Anderson was the Lutheran co-chair of the Lutheran-Roman Catholic Dialogue, the eighth round of which focused on the issue of "Justification." Eventually Anderson's leadership on the Lutheran-Catholic Dialogue helped to lead world Lutherans to the historic agreements with Roman Catholics signed in October 1999. As Presiding Bishop of the ELCA, Anderson presented the 1997 Luther College Annual Ecumenical Lecture on the *Joint Declaration*, together with a Roman Catholic colleague. Early in his time at Luther Anderson had also invited an international study group of the Lutheran World Federation, in which he was also very active, to the Luther campus for a week long meeting. This meeting effectively introduced the college community first-hand to the larger church at work in the world.

For many years, Luther College and the community of Decorah, Iowa, have fostered a very special ecumenical cooperation. That this place continues to be recognized as an unusually ecumenical community is due in no small part to extraordinary contributions of its ecumenical pioneers. Testimony to the importance—and the rarity—of the achievement was given recently by our Vocation Visitor, Dr. Theodor Dieter of the Ecumenical Research Institute in Strasbourg, France. While on the Luther campus for three weeks, Dieter attended the usual celebration of Ash Wednesday in the college's Center for Faith and Life and was deeply moved by what he saw: Lutherans and Catholics sharing not only the imposition of ashes, but also the Eucharist—separately, but at least in the same room. The sight gave him renewed hope that the sometimes grueling struggle to bring different faith traditions to significant agreement is worth it. I am very grateful to have had the opportunity to document this important development that continues to shape the life and vocation of this college of the Lutheran church, just as it continues to present a rare model of ecumenical cooperation in this country and abroad.

In his 2002 *Luther College: Who We Are*, professor emeritus Wilfred Bunge discusses what it means to be a college of the Lutheran Church and has these words to offer:

> ...Luther College is a college of the Evangelical Lutheran Church in America. That means that the Lutheran Church acts as host in inviting people to participate in the college's educational mission, which might be compared to a banquet, or feast...The college is a religiously pluralistic community;

> Lutheran in this case does not mean exclusive...If the "Lutheranness" of the Luther College community begins with the Lutheran Church as host, it also embraces all members of the community as mutual hosts...This sense of mutuality proceeds from the Christian tradition but it extends to all who come here to teach and learn.[2]

Building on its "Lutheranness," the college has followed its institutional vocation to build ecumenical community over its nearly 150 year history. This realization began early in the life of the institution, when it opened itself in the 1960s to Roman Catholics and began then to embrace them in a considered way, enriching the faith experiences of both groups.

In the ensuing years, it has deepened its commitment to ecumenicity by embracing members of many other Christian denominations and in recent years, opened itself even further, to embrace Muslims, Buddhists, and others who do not share a Christian faith. Following its vocation of ecumenism has challenged the institution to stretch, to question, and to grow throughout the years—it still does. But, Luther College would not be the college of the Church it is today without the experience of community building that seeks not only to include, but also to welcome other faith traditions. The dynamic among them has enriched the life of the institution and helped to shape its identity as the "Church in higher education."[3]

What has caused this small liberal arts college of the Church, and the community around it, to come to dwell on the cutting edge of ecumenicity, a model of ecumenical life sharing? Why did this happen in this tiny town in a relatively isolated corner of the upper Midwest? Some 400 years ago in Europe, as the world well knows, Roman Catholics and the followers of Martin Luther became enemies, hurling brickbats at each other that caused much bloodshed and stood for all the centuries down into our time. Their descendants who immigrated to this part of America brought with them not only their prayer books, but also their religious prejudices. Confident in the belief that Catholics and Lutherans of every time and place were destined to remain estranged, the new immigrants to the Decorah area nurtured the religious divide between them as carefully as they did their growing crops in the fields of this new land.

The Norwegian Lutherans were among the very first settlers in this area, as Luther College historian Leigh Jordahl recounted:

> Norwegian immigrants began large scale settlements in Winneshiek and Allamakee counties during the 1850's. They brought their Lutheran catechisms and hymnbooks with them...Decorah Lutheran Church was organized in 1863; in 1867 a parsonage, still in use as Campus House on the Luther campus, was built; and in 1873, the present site [of First Lutheran Church] on Upper Broadway was purchased. Already by then Decorah had become the symbolic center of Norwegian church life in America.[5]

About the same time as the Norwegian Lutherans—1851—, early Roman Catholic pioneers of the area settled in Decorah; they were "mostly Irish families."[6] In the first years, they had no resident priest; rather, the district was visited by missionary priests from some 70 miles away near Dubuque, until 1857, when St. Benedict Church was officially established by the Diocese of Dubuque. Like Norwegian Lutherans, their first concern was to erect a church building in which to gather for weekly worship.

Lawrence Hand, whose parents were among the first Catholic settlers in the area, wrote,

> "I was born in Decorah, Iowa, January 29, 1861.... I was baptized in my father's house, where Father Farrell lived and said Mass and administered the Sacraments to the faithful...Father C.J. Lowery...came to Decorah in 1863. He immediately set about the erection of a new Church. My father, (James Hand) being a stone mason by trade, helped to lay the stone which was hauled from McGregor, a distance of fifty miles, by the farmers of the vicinity.... The first Mass was celebrated in the new church in October 1864."[7]

Only about one mile separated the original St. Benedict Church, located on East Broadway, and the "Decorah Lutheran Church" (now renamed First Lutheran Church), which was erected on West Broadway in 1876. When the first St. Benedict Church was replaced in 1917 by the much larger building now in use on the corner of West Main Street and Court Street, the Catholic and Lutheran churches were only three *blocks* apart. By tradition and teaching, however, no one crossed the line between them, and the members of the parishes did not associate with each other. Despite their physical proximity, the two denominations maintained a great distance from each other.[8]

With the *aggiornamento* of the Second Vatican Council of the mid 1960s, the relationships between Catholics and Protestants worldwide began to warm. In this little Norwegian-Irish town of Northeast Iowa, where the two denominations had long worshipped and worked and lived apart, but right next to each other, the warming happened quite readily and rapidly. In those extraordinary days, Luther College led the way in extending hospitality to its Catholic neighbors. The president of the college invited the Roman Catholic archbishop to town, and the college entered into a faculty exchange with Roman Catholic St. John's University in Collegeville, Minnesota. A Benedictine monk gave the Baccalaureate Address at one of Luther's Commencement ceremonies, and one of the most popular courses offered at Luther College became "Catholic Life and Thought." Within a decade Luther had established a Chaplain for Catholic Students as part of its Campus Ministry staff, and begun to provide for regular Masses on campus as well.

The remarkable success of the Luther College experiment in the 1960s and 70s and its long lasting impact on both college and town, is directly attributable to the college's embrace of its institutional vocation, of its call to build ecumenical community. It flourishes for several reasons: the conscious integration of the exchange into the curricular structure of the institution, both in course offerings and in the spiritual life of the college, particularly daily chapel; and the continuous support of the college administration, with absolute public and personal commitment to the issue of ecumenism; as well as the effectiveness of the representatives, who became positive models for ecumenical living. For its time and place, the exchange represented a most forward-thinking vision of diversity, embraced by the community. As Wilfred Bunge observed in 2002, "An exchange of faculty between Catholic and Lutheran colleges wouldn't rate a blip on the screen of diversity today, but for those days it seemed extraordinary."[9]

Historian Leigh Jordahl noted,

> "The exchange program was only one instance of a purposeful ecumenicity that reflected the viewpoint of [Luther College president Elwin] Farwell and [academic dean] John Linnell. The word "ecumenical" used to describe their positions must be understood more broadly than only pertaining to the religious life. Both men believed in self-identity but were foes of the provinciality that too easily accompanies it. Both

men believed, in principle, that a college with a deeply rooted commitment to the liberal arts must, to avoid stagnation, cultivate diversity. As a community of faith and learning, Luther had nothing to fear from the stimulation that would come exactly from confronting new ideas.[10]

The Anderson administration, as committed as the last to such "purposeful ecumenicity" as the vocation of the institution, subsequently built on what had gone before. Before long, there was an international Lutheran conference on campus discussing ecumenical living, an archbishop and Lutheran campus pastor co-presiding over a service in the CFL, and a series of lectures on ecumenical dialogues that now embraces all the major world religions, including Islam, Buddhism, and Judaism.

Just before the beginning of the twenty-first century, an historic event occurred in Augsburg, Germany: the signing of the breakthrough document called the *Joint Declaration on the Doctrine of Justification*. This document between Roman Catholics and Lutherans all over the world was the first, and very significant step in ending several centuries of separation between the two church bodies, some of it very bloody. Though it does not mean that all disagreements between Catholics and Lutherans have been eliminated, it does mean that there has been tangible progress. It does mean that the two can make the miraculous claim, "Together we confess: By grace alone, in faith in Christ's saving work and not because of any merit on our part, we are accepted by God and receive the Holy Spirit, who renews our hearts while equipping and calling us to good works."[11]

The pages that follow tell the story of the extraordinary ecumenical call of Luther College through some of the voices of the people who have helped shape its ecumenical life over the past forty years. A number of reflections were written especially for this volume, including essays by Marilyn Roverud, Wilfred Bunge, and Fr. Gary Krapfl. The contributions of Bishop April Ulring Larson, Archbishop Jerome Hanus, Mark Muggli and Carol Gilberston, Theodor Dieter, and the author are homilies or addresses shared with the Luther College community in recent years.

Whatever the original form, each writer reflects on both gifts and challenges of living ecumenically within this college of the church, in Decorah where it is situated, and far beyond. What gathers the writers together is that they each have experienced a personal and profoundly moving encounter with ecumenism and the sense of institutional vocation at Luther College.

Ever committed to its strong Lutheran heritage, Luther College in recent years has begun to open itself to inter-religious conversations and to hear in them a welcome and fruitful dimension of diversity to its longtime ecumenical posture. As the vocation of ecumenism continues to grow and develop at Luther College, more than ever it will need the informed and committed voices of the community. This book is written so that students, past, present and future, may know the story and come to take their place in it.

*Soli Deo Gloria*

Ruth R. Kath
Luther College

Chapter One

# A Monk Teaching at Luther? BRAVO!

There is a little worn piece of paper among the archival treasures from the presidency of Dr. Elwin D. Farwell (1963–1981). It is a stunningly short letter from an alumnus of the class of 1909. Dated March 10, 1969, it says succinctly, "Sir: A monk teaching at Luther? A Lutheran, at St. John's?! I had not expected anything like that to happen in my life-time. BRAVO!"[12]

Dr. Elwin D. Farwell

Elwin Farwell claims that that brief note was one of the only responses he ever got to the extraordinary initiative he undertook in 1967, when he suddenly decided to exchange Religion faculty with St. John's University. "*BRAVO!*," indeed. Farwell himself could not have imagined at the time what a profound and lasting effect that direct exchange of Catholics and Lutherans would have on Luther College, and on its vocation as a Christian institution of higher learning. The small seed of harmony between Catholics and Lutherans on two college campuses would eventually blossom into national and international ecumenical engagement, unparalleled in this country.

From its founding, Luther College—even its name—was unmistakably Lutheran, as the Mission Statement of 1924–25 attests, "The chief aim of the College is to provide a liberal and thorough education for young men who intend later to enter the ministry."[13]

The *ministry* they were to enter after graduation was Lutheran—Norwegian Lutheran, to be specific. In the beginning, the faculty, staff, and students were all Lutheran. Its Bible requirement was Lutheran too, as were its required worship services, and daily chapel. Throughout the century following its founding, the College saw its aim as service to the Church. Yet, by the early 1960s, the understanding of Lutheranism was changing, and so was the world beyond the campus. The time was ripe for change, at Luther College and elsewhere in the world. The change came in surprising ways. In 1965, the Second Vatican Council had concluded its two-year meeting and called for reconciliation with other Christian churches. This revolutionary step opened the way for ecumenical cooperation. Luther College had already opened its doors to Roman Catholics well before that. Because the college fully embraced the changes around it, it would become a pioneer of ecumenical cooperation among church-related institutions.

At the helm of Luther College since early in 1963, President E.D. Farwell had been raised in the Baptist tradition. He was a devoted Lutheran pastor, an educator, and a man of extraordinary vision. The Second Vatican Council would not convene in Rome for another two years, but in the spring of 1963, shortly after his own arrival, Farwell invited Archbishop James Byrne of Dubuque, Iowa, to deliver a public lecture in Valders Hall of Science. Little is recorded of what the Archbishop said in his speech, but the impact of his short visit would be profound for both Lutherans and Catholics. As Will Bunge wrote, "It was a cordial and gracious visit on both sides. Archbishop Byrne expressed very positive feelings toward Luther College, because he considered Luther to be positive about religion, and he put his blessing on young Catholics coming to Luther as students."[14] The thoroughly Catholic archbishop might pay a courtesy visit to the new president of a neighboring college, but how could a Catholic archbishop recommend attending a Lutheran College? Farwell recalled hearing the archbishop say, "If all Catholic institutions took their faith as seriously as this one..."[15]

The precipitous juncture for people of vision to meet just three years later further sharpened the college's focus on its institutional calling to practice Lutheran hospitality in an ecumenical framework. Luther College historian Leigh Jordahl reflected in *Stability and Change:*

> *Aggiornomento* (a "bringing up to date") was the word used when Pope John XXIII called together the Second Vatican Council...The council itself is best known for a stress on

> ecumenicity hitherto little expected from Catholics. In Protestant circles, too, the 1960s became the great decade for moving from narrow denominationalism to ecumenical cooperation. Elwin Farwell fit the mood of the period. He was an optimist by nature and an ecumenist by conviction. He was convinced that Luther College should be a comfortable home for faculty and students from a wide variety of denominations.[16]

The one-day visit of the Catholic archbishop in 1963 foreshadowed both a long term and cutting-edge exchange of teaching theologians with a Catholic university beginning in 1967, and the unforeseen birth of a Catholic campus ministry at Luther College. As well as much lasting ecumenical cooperation among the churches in the Decorah area. When it came, the opening to Roman Catholics happened rapidly, resonated deeply, and profoundly altered the face of the Luther College campus, the student body, the campus ministry, and the department of Religion and Philosophy, as well as the churches of the town. Just over a decade later, in a 1974 letter to Byrne, Farwell reflected on those developments:

> We are...grateful to you for your support of a Catholic chaplain on our campus. You have provided a witness by your support to the actions taken by Vatican II. The Christian love that exists in Decorah among people of the various churches gives a positive evidence of the results of such Christian concern. I treasure the time that you came to our campus in April, 1963 shortly after I had joined this institution, and I would hope that sometime in the near future we might have you make another visit to Luther.[17]

> While Byrne himself never paid another visit, his successors did.

If the visit of Archbishop Byrne had opened the door in 1963, the real breakthrough came just three years later, as Luther College was making preparations to replace Preus Gymnasium, its largest gathering space and chapel, which had burned to the ground in 1961. The Center for Faith and Life on the Luther campus would eventually result from the preparatory research, but the work would have another, unexpected benefit. As the fact-finding committee, led by Luther College president Farwell, toured the upper Midwest, its focus was on edifices of other church-related colleges and universities of the area. What evolved from one such tour in the spring of 1967, was the unprecedented breakthrough that would further sharpen Luther College's vocation as a denominationally-based institution of higher learning that is called to ecumenicity:

> In the fall semester of 1966, a Luther College Chapel Building Committee, including then President Elwin Farwell, Robert Jenson of the religion faculty, and Gordon Smedsrud, campus pastor, visited St. John's University in Collegeville, Minnesota, to examine the new Abbey Church, completed in 1962. St. John's President Colman Barry invited them to dinner, and in the course of dinner conversation asked President Farwell whether he would consider an exchange of faculty theologians with St. John's. Father Colman was caught off guard by Farwell's quick response: "Sure, let's do it next year!"[18]

Farwell recalls being nearly as surprised as Colman Barry at the response he gave and woke up the next morning wondering to himself what he had done.[19] He had certainly not planned such a thing when he left Decorah that day. Actually, he and his two companions drove to see the newly built chapel at Gustavus Adolphus College in St. Peter, Minnesota. After that visit, they spontaneously decided to stop at Collegeville. Since it was late afternoon when they arrived, Barry invited the group to attend the 4PM worship in the new church and then to stay as guests for dinner. Ecumenism was already at work, even that day, while the Luther contingent did not take communion at the afternoon Mass, dinner itself appropriately included bread and wine, as Farwell vividly remembers. The ground-breaking connection had been established:

> Thus began a faculty exchange program which continued for seven years...and signaled a dramatic change in the ecumenical posture of Luther College, in the student body, and in relationships among churches in Decorah...It may in fact have promoted some of those changes...At the very least, the exchange marked or called attention to those changes.[20]

Despite perceptible surprise on both sides about the results of that spring visit in 1967, the exchange between Luther College and St. John's had not really emerged in a vacuum, but rather evolved from the kind of collaborative work to which Farwell dedicated himself throughout his presidency:

> Soon after he became Luther's sixth president in February, 1963, Farwell took the lead in developing a new association of

colleges, the Central States Colleges Association. One of the projects of this Association was faculty exchanges among the member colleges. Since St. John's and Luther were both members, Father Colman's suggestion of a faculty exchange in theology came out of CSCA as well as from ecumenical interests. It was the only long-term faculty exchange to develop among CSCA colleges; the other exchanges were typically several days in duration.[21]

The exchange of theologians between Luther College and St. John's University became one of the most markedly pragmatic and visible signs of unity among Lutherans and Catholics in the nation. While other colleges of the new association hosted faculty exchanges for only several days at a time, Luther College and St. John's University exchanged theologians for a whole academic year over an seven-year period. Bunge's assessment hints at the truth: The exchange certainly did both mark and call attention to those changes, but more than that, it promoted them in a careful and considered way. In fact, it might be said that the exchange anticipated by some thirty years the widespread ecumenical cooperation that would begin to develop among churches, schools and colleges after the 1999 signing of the *Joint Declaration on the Doctrine of Justification.* The joint endeavor between a Catholic and a Lutheran institution of higher learning was clearly far ahead of its time.

Given the more than 400-year animosity between Lutherans and Roman Catholics, the start of the exchange was challenging for both parties. However, before the year was out, members of both communities had begun to experience the strong connection between Catholics and Lutherans in the common commitment to liberal arts education, within the context of Christianity. There were many details to be worked out before the beginning of the exchange in the fall of 1967. The obvious ones included personnel on both ends, transportation, housing, teaching schedules, and costs. After some discussion, St. John's University proposed sending to Luther College Fr. Emeric Lawrence, O.S.B., who had taught French and religion for many years at St. John's.

The placing of a Roman Catholic monk/priest at Luther College involved garnering the support of Harris Kaasa, the young Head of the Religion and Philosophy department at Luther College. During Emeric Lawrence's preparatory visit to Luther in 1967, Kaasa became understandably concerned about the unassuming monk and his ability to take on the demanding role of initial exchangee from St. John's, as Will Bunge recalled:

> Harris was very uneasy when Emeric visited us in Spring 1967, shortly after I had been to St. John's. Emeric was so self-effacing that he had convinced Harris that there was virtually nothing that he could do. I reassured Harris that I had seen Emeric in his native country, that he was very much at ease there, that he had a nice sense of humor, that he was probably nervous about the move, and that once he got acquainted he would get on quite well and function quite effectively. I don't credit myself with being an outstanding instant judge of people, but in this case I think I did quite well.[22]

Emeric and Kaasa became the best of friends.

The monk's placement at Luther College also required the courtesy of clearing the arrangement with the Roman Catholic Archbishop of Dubuque, James Byrne, in whose diocese Decorah was located. Byrne had warm feelings about Luther College and its president because of the positive visit to the campus he had had before. Observing protocol, it was St. John's President Colman Barry who wrote the letter to Byrne, proposing the placement of Emeric Lawrence as a professor of Religion at Luther College. With enthusiasm, the Archbishop replied to him:

> I am very happy to give my wholehearted approval to Father Emeric Lawrence being exchange professor at Luther College during the 1967–68 year. The relations between Luther College and the Catholic Parish in Decorah have been excellent. President Farwell has done everything in his power to keep them that way. I assure you that the priests in the parish, in fact the priests in the entire area, feel very kindly towards President Farwell and Luther College.[23]

*Father Emeric Lawrence*

A similar letter of introduction was written by John Linnell, Academic Dean of Luther College, to Colman Barry, proposing Dr. Wilfred F. Bunge, Assistant Professor of Religion and Classical Languages at Luther

College, as the first exchangee to St. John's, just one year after completing his Harvard doctorate in New Testament Theology. Bunge's credentials were impeccable: he was a graduate of Luther College, where he had now taught for six years. He had teaching experience at both Luther Theological Seminary and Harvard Divinity School, he had recently completed his dissertation on "The Christology of Ignatius of Antioch," and could teach either classics, or religion.

In the fall of 1967, Bunge, his wife Ruth and their young son moved to Collegeville to begin the exchange. Because there was no suitable housing in Collegeville, the family lived in a furnished rental house in the city of St. Cloud, some distance from the campus. According to the written agreement forged between St. John's and Luther, each faculty exchangee was to continue drawing the usual salary from the home institution; the host institution provided moving expenses...Bunge recalls that the agreement worked reasonably well, but that housing nearer the university would have allowed more opportunity for integration into university life.

*Emeric Lawrence, Jerome Theisen, Wilfred Bunge*

At St. John's, Will Bunge taught survey courses in Bible to undergraduates, a graduate-level course on the Gospels, a second year Greek course and a section in the Great Books Honors Program. One of Bunge's young students in the freshman course was Mark Muggli, who would later become a professor of English at Luther College and one of Bunge's colleagues on the Luther College faculty.[24] Bunge also maintained an office within the Religion department on campus. However, his involvement with the life of St. John's was limited. Bunge was not considered part of the voting faculty. His closest faculty contacts were with lay faculty, who lived in other towns some distance away and commuted to the St. John's campus every day. Bunge did not preach at the St. John's church, nor did he participate in the daily Masses held there. All of this was a significant change from his life as a professor at Luther College.[25]

At the end of his exchange year in Collegeville, Bunge wrote an essay reflecting on his experience that was published in university alumni magazine *St. John's*. It was titled simply, "A Lutheran at St. John's" and focused less on the daily experiences of an exchangee than on the remarkable situation of the two church denominations coming together in that place:

> It can be said without much fear of contradiction that the Church is in a period of profound self-examination and change....The shift of interest from the ideological to the pragmatic is one way of describing the ecumenical explosion in the Church of our day. The Church has recognized her responsibility to be responsive to the world of which she is a part. This recognition has been experienced in universal terms, that is, the tasks of the Church are the tasks of all the churches. Surely this recognition of a common vocation, both in terms of the common Lord from whom the vocation comes and the common world toward which the vocation is directed, has driven us to seek more visible signs of unity to give expression to shared experience.[26]

Bunge was followed in the exchange in the 1968–69 academic year by Dale Johnson.[27] John Sieber, who had graduated from Luther College, and joined the college just four years before the start of the program represented Luther on the exchange in 1969–70.[28]

The practical issues of disruption for the family and housing located at a good distance from the campus that had complicated life for Wilfred Bunge and his family also challenged John Sieber, his wife and two children. Sieber recalled, "We were the third couple to go on the exchange and since we had two small children (Anne was 7, and Hans 3) it meant a lot of upheaval for the family. We lived the first month at the Ecumenical Institute and then had to move to an apartment in St. Joseph. I rode the commuter school bus from St. Benedict's [College] to St. John's and back most days, then walked about half a mile home."[29]

Despite this, in the two years since Bunge had begun the exchange, many details of daily ecumenical living had been worked out, including hospitality at daily meals, and worship. Sieber remembered, "The monks were exceptional hosts to me and to all of us. They invited me to eat often, let me participate in services from the [monks'] stalls [in the abbey church] and generally accepted me."[30]

The ensuing years of the exchange allowed a total of six members of the Luther College Religion department to spend a year teaching at St. John's University. An expansion of the teaching assignment for visiting Luther College faculty at St. John's emerged as among its most extraordinary ecumenical aspects. Bunge had begun the exchange by teaching basic scripture courses to St. John's undergraduates. Beginning with John Sieber in 1969, however, visiting Luther theologians taught courses in Theology and were also invited to participate fully in the team-taught seminar for first-year students in the Roman Catholic seminary at St. John's. John Sieber noted, "I taught a general introduction to Bible in the college, one section each semester....My main teaching was in the Seminary with two monks...we team taught a course that looked at four periods of church history and looked at those as case studies for the various theological disciplines. I mostly taught Bible (of course) but also some church history, ethics and other things."[31]

Having served the exchange during its fourth year, 1970–71, Joseph Everson reflected on his role as a Lutheran theologian in the Catholic university, "My arrival at St. John's coincided with a particularly optimistic and hopeful era in ecumenical relationships. St. John's had won a very prestigious Bush Foundation grant for scholarships for Protestant or other non-Catholic theologians. And more importantly, it was a time when the influence of the Second Vatican Council was reaching seminaries with a sense of openness and confidence."[3233]

The fact that Luther College exchangees like Everson stood before the classes of the School of Theology at St. John's University as committed Lutherans, lay or ordained, engendered some surprise on the part of the early seminary students. They had come to the Roman Catholic seminary expecting to encounter only priests and monks. Everson recalled their astonishment at his introduction:

> I taught Hebrew Bible/Old Testament in the Divinity School and was one of five faculty members appointed to oversee the formation of the first year priest formation class. I remember those experiences quite vividly because I was a Lutheran lay person, married, with two lively sons. At the opening reception, one first-year student questioned me up and down about my Lutheran background and my married state...and finally asked: "What are you doing here?" Needless to say, he was quite shocked to hear that I was going to be one of his five major teachers.[34]

Despite the shock Everson engendered among these first students, he completed a full academic year as exchange professor, and also continued to teach at St. John's during summers through 1976, well beyond the end of the exchange. Everson returned to Luther College each fall until 1975, when he took up a period of parish work in Minneapolis, before assuming a teaching position at California Lutheran University.

By the fifth year of the exchange, 1971–72, Luther College professor Bradley Hanson no longer encountered surprise in Collegeville. In fact, Hanson preached regularly in the St. John's Chapel, and at St. Benedict's College, and he participated fully in Eucharistic celebrations.[35] While at St. John's, Hanson taught in the first theology course in seminary, and participated in an orientation retreat with the seminarians. In the January term and the spring semester, he taught the seminarians alone.

Another major ecumenical aspect of the exchange was the development of a course that focused on the contrast between teachings of the two faith traditions. Together with recent exchangee Zachary Williams, O.S.B., Hanson developed and taught a new course for St. John's, and St. Benedict's undergraduates. The course was called *Lutheran and Catholic Thought Compared* and carried the following course description, "A comparison of the life and thought of the Lutheran and Catholic churches in their historical and sociological backgrounds, their basic beliefs and practices, and their present ecclesial situation."[36]

The new course was situated under Systematic Theology and began with the Reformation and a Catholic film which was somewhat critical of Martin Luther, as Bradley Hanson remembered. The course concluded with the Lutheran-Catholic Dialogue current at the time. The majority of the students were Catholic, but there were a few Protestants in the group, as he recalled. When Hanson returned to the Luther campus in the fall of 1973, the course was offered there in addition to the regular *Catholic Life and Thought* course that had been initiated by Fr. Emeric Lawrence in 1967.[3737]

As a result of his exchange year at St. John's and the contacts that Luther College professor Joseph Everson continued to make among his summer school students there, he eventually initiated an ecumenical January Term course in the Bahamas. From his current teaching post at California Lutheran University, Everson remembered the beginning of the innovative course in this way:

> Among [my most excellent students in the summer school sessions at St. John's] were several Bahamian sisters from a convent in Nassau...they asked if I had ever visited Nassau. If I could come, they expressed the hope that I might teach a course for the sisters at their convent. That was the beginning! Back at Luther and facing another fierce winter season, I kept thinking about January in Nassau. So I wrote a proposal to Dr. John Linnell, who was then our academic dean. I heard later that he was reviewing a stack of papers as he and three other faculty or administrators were driving to Madison, Wisconsin for some college meeting. According to a friend, he exclaimed: "Listen to this, we have a faculty member who is actually asking for funding so that he can spend time in the Bahamas during January!" My grant request was approved; I spent several weeks in Nassau visiting Roman Catholic elementary and secondary schools; I stayed at St. Augustine's monastery which was a mission of St. John's and I taught in the local Benedictine monastery.[3839]

After Everson's preparatory trip to the Bahamas in 1973, he and a Catholic co-leader from St. John's took approximately fifteen students there in January 1974 and 1975. The students drawn from Luther College, St. John's and St. Benedict's College. In 1974, Fr. Zachary Williams, O.S.B. co-led the course with Everson, and in 1975, it was Fr. Emeric Lawrence, O.S.B., in his sixth and final year of ecumenical residence at Luther College. Joseph Everson recalled both the articulated intent of the course and the gratifying effect of the students' presence in the developing nation:

> For the next several years, we brought Luther students to the Bahamas, placing them as student assistants in various schools. Our stated goal was to introduce both white and black U.S. students to life in a predominantly black culture. Most were students who were thinking about teaching; without exception, those who were planning careers in physical education were welcomed and celebrated as local teachers stood in awe at what they were doing during the traditional recess times. Very few of those teachers had any training in physical education or exercise therapy.[40]

The Bahamian outreach during the January Terms 1973–75, also bore fruit back at Luther College, contributing to the international diversity of the campus, as Everson recalled:

> We were there during the time when the Bahamas gained their independence from England, and the end of colonization was highly celebrated. What was really telling was that during the time of British rule, no one had thought about higher education for the Bahamas. When we were there, there was still not a single college or university in the Bahamas. So I was particularly delighted when Barbara Thompson was the first Bahamian student to enroll at Luther. Many, of course, had come to St. John's and other U.S. schools. A number of other Bahamian students followed Barbara to Luther....[Registrar] Ruth Mostrom was invited to the Bahamas by later Bahamian students.[41]

The final exchangee sent by Luther College to St. John's was John Helgeland. Helgeland served the sixth and seventh year of the exchange, during the 1972–73 and 1973–74 academic years. Helgeland had been at Luther for a year on a short-term appointment, and because of longstanding staffing commitments, Helgeland's move to Collegeville was made without prospect of returning to Luther. The exchange ended officially in 1974. However, the popular Helgeland continued to teach at St. John's until the end of the 1976–77 academic year, when he joined the faculty of North Dakota State University. [42]

The first exchangee sent by St. John's University to Luther College was, of course, Fr. Emeric Lawrence, O.S.B. In the second year of the exchange, Emeric returned to Luther. In the third year, the delegate was Fr. Daniel Durken, O.S.B., who arrived on the Luther campus in the fall of 1969. Durken's quiet warmth and dry wit endeared him to those who met him. In general, he kept a much lower profile on the campus and in the town than had his predecessor. As Emeric had, Durken lived in the apartment behind St. Benedict Church, and also helped out with Masses there, but Durken confined his campus activities otherwise to teaching classes and holding office hours. Durken was not involved in campus ministry and did not hold Mass on campus, although he did take his regular turn in preaching at chapel, as did the other professors of Religion. With characteristic humor, Durken remembered his initial contribution in that venue:

> Teaching full time at Luther College in Decorah, Iowa, was the best of times as I saw ecumenism at work among my colleagues and students. I had a hand in improving Lutheran-Catholic relations the first time I led the daily chapel service. It was the birthday of Pope Paul VI. So I asked the congrega-

tion to sing "Happy Birthday" to the pope. They did so—a little tentatively. And Martin Luther probably took another turn in his grave.[43]

Even some thirty years later, Durken still remembered his year at Luther College as "remarkable."[44]

Durken was followed at Luther in 1970–71 by Zachary Williams, O.S.B.[45] During the fifth year, Hanson's exchange partner from St. John's was none other than Fr. Emeric Lawrence, returning for a third time to the Luther campus. In 1972–73, St. John's sent Jerome Theisen, O.S.B., as the exchange professor, as well as Emeric Lawrence as the chaplain to Catholic students.[46] Like his predecessors, Theisen taught courses in Religion and in Freshman Studies, preached regularly in chapel, and helped out at St. Benedict Church. Theisen also team taught with Brad Hanson in the *Lutheran and Catholic Thought Compared* that Hanson and Zachary Williams had offered together at St. John's the year before. Fr. Emeric returned to Luther College for a sixth year in 1973–74 and served as both chaplain to the Catholic community, and exchange professor until the program ended.

The priest-monks who came to Luther College from St. John's University found at the college a deep commitment to the Scripture commonly shared, the practice of setting aside time during the school day to worship, and a liturgy not much different from that of their own tradition. With the added support of the town parish and of their colleagues on campus, they soon felt at home and were able to function effectively. The exchangees who had been sent to St. John's returned to Decorah, one after another, with increased respect for the mystery of things Catholic: the beauty and dignity of the liturgy and ritual, as well as some appreciation for the bond, as well as the challenges, that characterize monastic living. They also returned with an understanding that, for all the surface differences, teaching students of the two faith traditions was not such a radically different enterprise from one place to another. For the most part, the students came from similar backgrounds and had much the same needs of teaching, caring, and thought-provoking guidance in each place.

Besides its ongoing daily work on both campuses, the exchange prompted a number of high-profile ecumenical events between the two institutions. In the fall of 1967, Fr. Colman Barry, O.S.B., was the chapel speaker for Reformation Day, and the following spring, Luther College students were invited to sing at the dedication ceremonies for the new Science Hall on the St. John's campus. Having already been named an Honorary Alumnus of Luther College Fr. Emeric Lawrence, O.S.B., was the invited speaker for the Baccalaureate Service in 1969. Well after the termination of the exchange, Father Colman Barry received an Honorary Degree from Luther College at the Senior Awards Day on May 15, 1981. At the St. John's commencement ceremonies that same year, E.D. Farwell was given an Honorary degree from St. John's.[47]

The extraordinary seven-year exchange of theologians between Luther College and St. John's University that had explored so many new ideas about ecumenical cooperation did indeed end. However, as Emeric Lawrence observed in a letter to Archbishop Byrne on December 12, 1974, the experiment had made more than made its mark, on the institutions, their faculty, staff, and students, and, most of all, on those chosen few who had participated in the ecumenical endeavor as exchangees. Emeric wrote:

> It is now seven and a half years since you first welcomed me into the Archdiocese of Dubuque as the first exchange professor of religion at Luther College. I think the exchange of professors between Luther and St. John's has been a very enriching experience for both colleges. For my part, these have surely been the most gratifying years of my priestly career of almost forty years.[48]

## Children of the Same Heavenly Father

**Marilyn Roverud '66**
Luther College Board of Regents

Moving from the farm to a new community was both exciting, and frightening. Leaving behind my third grade class in the middle of winter, and having to meet new classmates filled me with questions. What will the teacher be like? Will I make new friends? Will I like this new home? Will there be children my age in the neighborhood?

We were welcomed as a family, warmly. Neighbors knocked on our door, bringing us food, and introducing themselves. And yes, there were many children close to my age. One family had a girl *exactly* my age, and a boy *exactly* the age of my younger brother. From the very start we were nearly inseparable. Her name was Colleen Corcoran; her black hair, peaches and cream skin, and brown eyes fit her Irish name. Third grade for Colleen had been filled with changes as well. Her father had died suddenly in December, leaving her mother a widow with six children to raise. For Colleen, too, having a new friend was exciting and added some joy during a period of extreme sadness.

*Colleen Corcoran and Marilyn Roverud*

We did not go to the same school. Colleen attended the Catholic school, and I the public school. We spent our free time playing together; and when the winter snows melted and gave way to spring, we would ride our bikes. One day we rode to her church because she wanted to say a prayer for her dad. I went along. (In our hometown there was an understood segregation of Catholics and Protestants...two schools, two grocery stores, two doctors, two funeral homes, two cemeteries.) I waited in the entry as she dipped her finger in the holy water, and made the sign of the cross before entering the nave. I watched from the doorway and breathed in the smells of incense, and candle wax as she covered her head with a scarf and proceeded to go and kneel by some burning candles. When she returned to where I was standing, she told me that she had offered a prayer so that her father would not stay in purgatory. PURGATORY! What was that? I had never heard of such a place. You see, I was a Lutheran. I was as much a blond, blue-eyed and fair-skinned Norwegian Lutheran as she was an Irish Catholic. My ecumenical experience began with that bike ride.

We asked each other, and certainly our families, other questions. Why this? Why that? Why was her Lord's Prayer shorter? Why did she pray to Mary? Why did they have a Pope? Why were only Catholics saved, and was I really going to Hell? She explained about her rosary, the medal she wore on the chain around her neck, her first communion, her saints, and saints' days, and the very special May Procession in honor of the Blessed Mother. I observed holy water in her home, crucifixes on her family's walls, dried palms arching over pictures of Jesus, whose chest wall opened to reveal his heart. For her, there were fast days and meatless Friday. From a devout Catholic family, Colleen had uncles and aunts who were priests and nuns. Faith and service to the church were givens. The church, above all, gave her family its identity.

The same was true for my family. My Norwegian grandmother never sat down for a snack without saying a Norwegian prayer first. She read daily from her Norwegian prayer book, reciting prayers when she rose in the morning and when she went to bed at night. My parents taught us to pray as soon as we could talk—prayers at bedtime and prayers before meals. We read bible stories aloud, learning the stories of our faith. Attending church, singing in the choir, and serving in the church were at the heart of my family's faith and life—promises made at baptism, and treasured.

My family observed and experienced the changing Catholic Church with five Corcoran weddings. The first wedding was soon after we arrived. We were not invited. The second wedding included us. It was a High Mass in Latin, and we sat in the back of the church with no service book to follow. The third wedding was also in Latin, but we were given the missal in order to follow the service. The fourth wedding was in English and we were again given the missal and encouraged as guests to participate. Communion was celebrated at all of the weddings, but we were not invited to the table.

Colleen's wedding was the fifth in her family. She had gone to a Catholic college. I had gone to a Lutheran one. She entered the Peace Corps and met Tom, her future husband in Liberia while working in a well-baby clinic, and leper colony. Before she left for Africa, she was given a special dispensation to be a bridesmaid in my wedding in my Lutheran home congregation. A communion service for the wedding party and families was held at the close of our wedding rehearsal and Colleen chose to participate in that holy meal. It was a privilege for both of us to not only share communion but to share such a special lifetime event.

When Colleen and Tom set their wedding date, we were determined to attend. Colleen's service was a guitar Mass in English, and we were warmly invited to participate in the worship service and then to celebrate communion. How far we had come! From fears about purgatory and her tears that I would burn in Hell because I wasn't Catholic, to sharing the body, and blood of our Lord Jesus Christ in her church.

As lifelong friends—from early childhood to the present—we have shared everything from bicycle rides, swimming and diving experiences, and double dates, to our weddings, the births of our daughters, the deaths of our parents, and most recently the death of her husband. Throughout our lives, our faith has been our center—a wellspring in joy and in tragedy. At the same time, a mutual respect for our different faiths has deepened our relationship.

And today? I thank God for Colleen and all that I have learned from her. My faith has been strengthened and my life richly blessed by her friendship. For both of us, I am sure, our unique personal exploration of ecumenism has been a gift. Together, we are able to celebrate the greatest gift of all: the Birth, Death, and Resurrection of our Lord Jesus Christ. For in our baptism, we were both made children of the same heavenly Father and sealed with the cross of Christ forever. Of this, I am certain.

Thanks be to God!

Chapter Two

# Emeric's "Epistle to the Romans"

One Sunday morning very late in the last century, a wizened old man shuffled into the sacristy of St. Benedict Church in Decorah, Iowa, opened the priest's vesting case and proceeded to pull out clerical garments from the drawer, and drape himself in them with a flourish. I was the sacristan on duty for the day, but no one had warned me that this fellow was coming. It turned out to be fine: Fr. Emeric Lawrence, O.S.B. had come once again from Collegeville, Minnesota to visit his old Luther College friends and St. Benedict Church. He knew his way around very well.

That day in the late nineties, Fr. Emeric needed help from the resident pastor to get to his altar chair and then to the microphone for the sermon he preached that morning. He was getting old, and had already lost much of his sight, but what a treat he offered me that day: During the Mass that morning, I saw an exquisite picture from the sacristy: the bent, old man with balding head, and thick glasses that could no longer help him see, and a tall, young man with ruddy skin, and curly hair who had inherited the older one's treasured roles as priest, professor, and Chaplain to the Catholic students of Luther College.

The extraordinary picture that Sunday reminded me what the aging monk had done for Luther College while in Decorah more than two decades earlier. I wanted to express my appreciation for his pioneering work in a way that would mean the most to him. After the Mass concluded, and just before he headed out again, I guided him gently over to my worktable to tell him what I had been doing the whole hour. I showed him the old rewired telephone on the sacristy desk and told him, "This is the dial-up system for the live broadcast this morning—every Sunday the St. Benedict's Mass goes out live over the Luther College radio." He shook his head in quiet amazement and marveled that yet another bridge had been built between the Lutherans and Catholics where he had lived and worked with such effectiveness. Visibly moved, he shuffled off out of the room. My new-old friend Fr. Emeric Lawrence, O.S.B. would die within months of that memorable morning, but the ecumenical legacy he left to Luther College and the Decorah community lives on in the many who carry on the work, encouraging unity among Christians.

Father Emeric Lawrence

What difference had the dedicated Benedictine monk made to the institutional life of the committed Lutheran college in a corner of northeast Iowa? A tremendous one. Emeric Lawrence had paid two major visits to Luther College over the six years he was in residence there: one visit had begun in 1967, and lasted for two years; the second had started in 1971, and lasted for four. A third stay in Decorah in 1984 was for the spring semester only, and involved no teaching. Following his retirement, Fr. Emeric continued to visit Decorah on occasion, as on the morning above, whenever he could convince someone to drive him the some four hours southward from Collegeville.

Fr. Emeric Lawrence had not always been so anxious to go to Decorah. The first time he came, in fact, he was very reluctant. Why would a thoroughly Roman Catholic Benedictine monk want to take up residence at a thoroughly Lutheran college in a heavily Lutheran community such as Decorah, Iowa?

Despite his own understandable apprehensions about taking up residence on a Lutheran campus, Fr. Emeric was warmly received on the Luther campus from the first day, and he became fast friends with Catholics and Lutherans alike. He assisted with Masses at St. Benedict Church, participated in the life of Luther College, and its department of Religion and Philosophy, and introduced a popular new course for Lutheran students, "Catholic Life and Thought."

Having been made a full member of the Religion faculty, Emeric was expected to preach regularly at daily chapel. Despite his practice of daily Mass throughout his priestly life, he found this form of worship to be a new experience, and in his Journal entry on Monday, September 19, 1967, he recorded his first impressions, with characteristic tongue-in-cheek:

> Today, for the first time in my life, I preached to an audience that was almost 100% non-Catholic (although it is impossible to tell how many Catholics listened to the sermon over the college and city radio station). It was the daily chapel service of the college.... After my chapel sermon...several girls said to me: "oh, we thought your message was just wonderful!" It was the first time in my life that a sermon of mine had been called a "message."[49]

It must have been a singular sight on the campus of a committed Lutheran college to see a Roman collar preaching from the pulpit during daily chapel in 1967. But it must have been much more of a shock to see a Catholic Mass celebrated on the Lutheran campus later that fall. How did that happen? Will Bunge met Emeric Lawrence when he visited St. John's University prior to the first exchange in 1967, he was delighted by his personality, but puzzled by his most pressing question, "'Will I be able to celebrate Mass on campus?' I replied something to the effect that it wasn't really for me to say, but I knew no reason why he couldn't do so, all the while wondering why he would want to; I wasn't sure that we had any Catholic students."[50]

Indeed, there may not have been many Catholic students at Luther College that year, but, with the arrival of Fr. Emeric Lawrence on the campus, that demographic would soon be radically altered. The time was right, and the groundwork had been carefully, if unknowingly, laid for such a change. In the spring of 1963, when Archbishop Byrne had been invited to deliver a lecture at Luther College, there had been just three Catholic students enrolled, up from only one the previous year.[51] In the fall of 1967, when the St. John's exchange began, there were approximately a dozen Catholic students on the Luther campus, but not only Catholic students contributed to the success of the ecumenical exchange; there were many Lutheran ones, a good number of whom were apparently quite curious about Catholicism, in the years just following the conclusion of the Second Vatican Council.

Some sixty Lutheran students enrolled in Emeric's upper-division "Catholic Life and Thought" course the first fall of his Decorah residency. Over eighty students enrolled the following spring.[52] Part of the requirement for the course was that all students—even the Lutheran ones—subscribe to the Roman Catholic weekly newspaper, "The Witness," published by the Archdiocese of Dubuque, Iowa.[53] Students were asked to react in their journals to selected articles from the newspaper, including the regular column written by Fr. Richard C. McBrien of Notre Dame University.

From the beginning, the content of the course was a subject of constant debate among those enrolled. While students apparently expected that it would explicitly compare the two faiths, Emeric took a different approach which probably required more active reflection from the students about the subject, saying, "...I was convinced that in the long run it was more important for them as Protestants to know what Catholics believe and practice than for them to know about the differences between the two faiths...It has helped when I reminded them that the title of the course is 'Catholic Life and Thought.'"[54]

As Fr. Emeric soon learned, the young people at Luther College were not so terribly different from the young people at his St. John's University, and yet, he began to realize the enormous task of reconciliation to which he had been called. After the first week teaching at Luther College, Emeric had already gained some insight into the situation and remarked in his Journals:

> I had to conclude that some Lutheran students have as much difficulty believing in God as some Catholics. Then, too, it also seems to me that the thinking of Protestants is considerably different from the thinking of Roman Catholics. We are so close to each other in many ways....Nevertheless, some 400 years of separation have had their impact on both Protestants and Catholics, and I cannot but feel that in many ways there is a rather violent and very deep chasm between my thinking as a Roman Catholic and theirs as Protestants.[55]

Since its founding in 1861, there had never been anything but Lutheran worship services on the Luther College campus. Until 1956, Lutheran daily Chapel had been required for all students and faculty. Yet, as it emerged, it was precisely for the *Lutheran* students of his course "Catholic Life and Thought" that Fr. Emeric celebrated the first Mass on the Luther College campus.[56]

An extraordinary event in Luther College's ecumenical history occurred on an ordinary class day, on Thursday, November 21, 1967, within the context of the course. The occasion presented an unexpectedly teachable moment and Emeric was very pleased with the outcome, as he reflected afterward:

> Today, for the first time in history, a Catholic Mass was celebrated on the campus of Luther College. It also happened to be the feast of the Presentation of our Lady in the Temple. I wondered aloud about the ways of Divine Providence arranging that the first Mass at Luther should be one honoring the Mother of Jesus...I explained everything as we went along and was delighted at the enthusiasm with which they answered the prayers (of course, they all had misselettes borrowed from the parish church).[57]

The first event must certainly have been memorable, but it would take several more years for the practice of holding a Catholic Mass on the Luther campus to become regularized for the growing number of Catholic students enrolling at Luther College. Yet, Emeric Lawrence had set the process in motion and used an innovative way to teach about Catholicism. In breaking through century-old prejudice, however, at least for students at this Lutheran college, Fr. Emeric was unexpectedly troubled by something that had happened in the first worship encounter he had so carefully constructed for them. He reflected:

> One of the things that saddened me was that I alone received Communion. One of the girls asked me afterwards: "Why couldn't I receive Communion?" I quoted to her from the chapter on the Mass in our text which goes: "For the Catholic theologian inter-Communion must mean first of all a sharing of the understanding of what Communion means." I told her that Communion is this sign of unity, but I've never been really satisfied with that answer. Nor am I completely at ease with the observation that non-Lutherans are not welcome to receive Communion in some Lutheran congregations. To celebrate the Eucharist for a class, most of whom have become close friends, and not to be able to invite them to share the fruits of the Sacrifice, Holy Communion, is already a real agony for me.[58]

The distress over the lack of intercommunion with his students would continue for some time. Still, Emeric seems to have been fully aware of how to deal with it, at least professionally. In spite of the obvious differences in language and audience, Fr. Emeric found much that was familiar about the place: the people, the landscape, and the seriousness with which Luther College took its faith commitment. Particularly among his colleagues in the Religion department, he encountered some rumblings about a lack of a chapel at Luther College, yet he seems hardly to have missed what was so prominent at his own St. John's University: a place devoted solely to worship:

> The fact that there is no chapel at the college is a cause of regret and even embarrassment for many of the faculty, especially those in the religion department. But again the religious background and philosophy of the school is indicated by the fact that the entire operation, classes and administration, closes down for forty minutes each morning for the daily chapel service which is conducted in the gymnasium and broadcast over the college radio station....Each of the members of the religion department, myself included, take turns conducting the service, which consists usually of a scripture reading, a hymn, a short sermon, a prayer and a final hymn. I have tried to console those who envy St. John's its beautiful church with the reflection that the building of a community of worship and of scholars, while it can be helped by a building, by no means depends on it. Luther has maintained a religious atmosphere and a definite Christian spirit despite the absence of a chapel.[59]

The first two years of Emeric's Luther residency were devoted to ecumenical outreach, as he himself noted in his journals.[60] At St. Benedict Church, where he lived and helped out, he fit in with the other priests, but when he came to the Luther campus every day, he was almost exotic in his Roman collar and used his conspicuous presence to educate those with whom he came in contact there. In the classroom, he taught—directly or indirectly—about ecumenism, and when he preached regularly in the Luther College chapel, his favorite topic was the similarities between Catholic and Lutheran practices. Even in the pulpit of St. Benedict Church and in the occasional small Mass on campus, his homilies in those days were most likely to be on the importance of the ecumenical movement. While he seems to have reveled in his unique new standing as a Catholic clergyman called by Luther College to work ecumenically among Lutherans, the position also pushed him personally:

> It could be that I am the first priest to have taught full time in a Lutheran college. When people ask me where I am from and I answer, "Luther College," they do not quite know whether to take me seriously or not. Explanation about the exchange program of professors between St. John's and other members of the Central States College Association, together with awareness that there is indeed an ecumenical movement afoot reassures them somewhat. But more than once I have received the impression that I am on dangerous ground. The nervous question, "Are you married yet?" is only half a joke in the minds of many.
>
> Another frequent inquiry is about the number of converts I have made. I am not sure that my disclaimer of any intention to make converts is very convincing or satisfying to Catholic friends and even fellow priests. The early idea of the only ecumenical movement as crossing the street to the Catholic rectory dies hard, and any thought of concessions to be made by the Church or mistakes to be admitted is still foreign to the minds of many Catholics I have talked to.[61]

Clearly, the ecumenical work that Luther College had called him to do on the Lutheran college campus put him in a challenging position not only among the Lutherans he encountered in Decorah, but also among Catholics priests and parishioners wherever he went.

While he was teaching about Catholicism in those first two years at Luther College, Fr. Emeric also spent much time in outreach to the community of Decorah, speaking on ecumenism and helping to foster dialogue. Right on the heels of Vatican II, ecumenical cooperation was a very popular topic, and Emeric was in great demand as a speaker and facilitator. His work with the cooperation between St. Benedict and First Lutheran churches is of particular note and paralleled the innovative ecumenical work he had been undertaking at Luther College:

> [T]his spring...two meetings...assembled the members of Decorah's St. Benedict's parish and First Lutheran. A lay committee of First Lutheran was responsible for the content and format of the meetings. The first session consisted of a demonstration of the Mass in detail, followed by a panel discussion of the Eucharist between two ministers and two of us priests. The second was a talk on the points of difference and similarity between Lutherans and Catholics, again followed by discussion and questions. For me personally it was one of

> the high points of the year. The enthusiasm of the members of both parishes was that gratifying. The meetings will surely continue in years to come.[62]

Fr. Emeric's winning personality, coupled with the broad range of roles he played in those years, as professor of religion and local parish priest and increasingly, as a chaplain on the campus, allowed him to stay afloat on the uncharted waters he had entered by coming to Decorah. He was having a significant impact on the Lutheran campus and in the Decorah community:

> The old scorn and distrust—of which our ancestors on both sides were equally guilty—have pretty well disappeared. These days it is no longer difficult to convince anyone that hating one another in the name of Christ is a shocking and scandalous way to live out one's Christianity. I think that most of the residents of Decorah, Iowa, who were at first amazed at the presence of a Catholic priest on the Luther College campus, not only accept the fact but approve the principle.[63]

The St. John's-Luther College exchange of theologians clearly enjoyed the full support of both college administrations. Eventually each president would receive an honorary degree from the other's college, but institutional support was already evident in the first year of the exchange. On Reformation Day 1967, Fr. Colman Barry, O.S.B., appeared at Luther College to be the chapel speaker. While institutional enthusiasm was high, the occasion also pointed out the painful need to grow in ecumenical sensitivity toward each other, as Emeric Lawrence recalled in his Journal:

> Last Wednesday Father Colman Barry, President of St. John's, gave the festive Reformation Day address to faculty, students and the neighboring countryside (via radio). Fr. Colman's manner—a happy blending of humor and scholarship—won him considerable applause.... However, towards the end of his speech he made reference to the Gospel parable of the Prodigal Son, and those who wished to could draw the conclusion that the prodigal son who departed their father's house were Luther and the reformers. Afterwards one of the members of the faculty commented that it was a very fine speech but that he was really not accustomed to thinking of himself as a prodigal son.[64]

By the end of the first year of the exchange both the Luther College and St. John's University communities were counting the undertaking a singular success. Each institution declared itself ready, able and most willing to continue the effort. In an article for the *St. John's Magazine* written just at the end of the first exchange, Fr. Emeric reflected on the fruits of the past year and looked ahead to the future:

> There is every reason to hope that the exchange of professors between Luther College and St. John's will be the beginning of a movement that is bound to grow and enrich more and more religiously-based colleges. Catholic and Protestant clergy and laity alike are realizing that disunity is a shocking scandal and that something has to be done about it. I think I was able to share my convictions on this matter of unity with most of my students at Luther, and if that conviction remains with them and prompts them to further discussion and study, the year will have been happily worthwhile.[65]

Thoroughly convinced of the success of the new exchange, Luther College had been very ready to continue the second year, this time with a nun from St. Benedict College, the sister institution to St. John's University. Unfortunately, the sister suffered a broken hip and became unable to travel, so Emeric Lawrence was invited to return for a second year to continue the work he had begun. By the end of the second year of the exchange, however, it became clear that Fr. Emeric would move on to similar work at Concordia College in Moorhead, Minnesota.

At the 1969 ceremony Fr. Emeric not only gave the Baccalaureate Address, he was also made an honorary alumnus of the college. Not surprisingly, Emeric's message to the graduating class that year focused on Christian unity and understanding and issued an invitation to them to join him in the effort to bring them about:

> We are Christians. We believe in the same Christ, we accept the same Gospel. But we are separated in our interpretation of that Gospel; and very often in the past this division has manifested itself in attitudes, words and actions that might cause historians to question if the Gospel ever did penetrate and transform our minds and hearts. Chris-

> tians have despised and hated one another in the name of Christ, in the name of that Jesus who in his life and words presented unity and fraternal love as the one mark of discipleship.
>
> To me this division is a scandalous and an evil condition. If I love Christ, I cannot think otherwise; and for as long as I live and can teach and preach, I shall do what I can to make all my fellow Christians aware of the unreasonableness of this condition....I invite all of you, but especially you graduates, to make the cause of unity your own.[66]

In accepting the invitations of Luther College, Emeric Lawrence had found a surprising new calling late in life: ecumenical work. Following the two years at Luther, Emeric spent two additional years at Concordia College, Moorhead, Minnesota. During that time, he formulated what he had learned about teaching about Catholicism at Luther College into a book about Catholics and Lutherans, *Understanding Our Neighbor's Faith.* Emeric would use his little book of explanation to teach Luther College students in his courses on his return to the campus on his second major visit beginning in 1971. Yet, even while he was absent, Luther College maintained a strong connection to him, awarding him a Distinguished Service Award in 1970.

Following his return to Luther College for his second major visit beginning in 1971, Emeric acquired an additional—or sometimes, substitute—responsibility at the college, that of chaplain to the Catholic students. By that time, the number of Catholics enrolled at Luther College had grown significantly. The appointment came about because, "a considerable number of students and faculty thought that it would be a good idea to have a chaplain for the hundred or more Catholic students on campus and that Luther College could stand two priests," as Emeric himself modestly recalled.[67] In a later tribute to Fr. Emeric, Luther Religion professor Bruce Wrightsman recalled the incident this way:

> ...Three or four years ago, when [Fr. Emeric] was about to leave us, a few students spontaneously started a petition to President Farwell and to the Abbot of St. John's pleading to let [Fr. Emeric] stay. Now, you should know that no petition circulating on this campus during the last eight years, even at the height of student outrage against the war in Vietnam, ever drew more than 300 signatures. But this one was signed by nearly 800 students, faculty and staff![68]

As a result of the extraordinary petition, the popular Fr. Emeric was invited by the Luther College administration to stay on in a newly created position as part time chaplain for Catholic students, in addition to part-time work as a professor of Religion. He was joined at Luther College by his St. John's *confrere*, Fr. Jerome Theisen, who spent the year as the full time exchange professor.[69] That year, the Religion department faculty of Luther College included not just one priest, but two. After that, Emeric held both positions simultaneously through the conclusion of the exchange in 1975.

As Catholic chaplain appointed by the administration of a distinctly Lutheran college, Emeric devoted considerable energy and time to his collegiate congregation. As their pastor, he felt himself more and more to be the special representative of the Catholic Church on the campus and felt a responsibility to provide for his people a Catholic environment and presence on the Lutheran campus. "[T]he spiritual welfare of my tiny flock became my deepest preoccupation. They will never know how responsible I felt for their welfare—academic, physical and emotional, but above all spiritual. They provided a pastoral dimension to my priestly life, and I shall be forever grateful to them."[70]

Upon his return to the Luther campus, Emeric quickly made Mass on campus a regular weekly event. Though others were regularly invited to participate, it was unmistakably a Catholic service. He involved the Catholic students in planning, and tailored the Mass to their tastes in music and worship. He worried only mildly that he was spoiling them for their own home parishes. The Catholic community that had blossomed at his first arrival was now flourishing under his so-called "second coming," and Emeric Lawrence was justifiably proud about the developments that his presence had precipitated on the Luther College campus. In his journals, he reflected on the growth that had taken place in the Catholic community since he had first come to Decorah:

> During the first years of the St. John's priests' presence on campus, we chose to invite—and even sent cars to campus to pick up—Catholic students to attend Mass at St. Benedict's parish church in Decorah. Not too many took advantage of the opportunity, but those who did were a great help with the music at the main parish Mass. Upon my return in 1971 I decided to make Sunday (and occasionally weekday) Mass more available and arranged to celebrate the Eucharist in a large room in the student union overlooking the lovely Upper Iowa

River valley. I used to call this our Cathedral in the Sky and often wonder aloud if any other college could boast of a more beautiful "Chapel."[71]

Beginning in the early 1970's Emeric Lawrence sent each of the Catholic students a weekly missive that he called *Emeric's Epistle to the Romans*. It covered a full page or more and contained a message of greeting, a summary of the week's preaching, reminders about the Masses and other activities coming up, recommendations about a new movie or book, as well as the occasional funny story. The chatty letter with its distinctive typeface soon became a familiar sight in the students' post office boxes. Besides the weekly Sunday Mass, Emeric held a weekday Mass on Mondays and Fridays at 5PM and on Wednesdays at 7PM. In addition, he invited the students to call him anytime of the day or night for confessions or anything else.[72]

While Emeric continued to lobby hard for cooperation and understanding between Catholics and Lutherans, he became painfully aware of a seemingly insurmountable obstacle to Christian unity: the perilous so-called "mixed marriages" between Lutherans and Catholics. The concern apparently arose from conversations with his Catholic students enrolled at Luther College, especially those who anticipated leaving Catholicism behind when they entered a mixed marriage. The question strained his ecumenical spirit to a breaking point, and he began to doubt the wisdom of his having gone to Luther College at all. Though he had long since learned to negotiate a way around the divided Eucharist, he could not find a solution to this problem:

> What worried me is not that the young people would learn anything contrary to their beliefs, not that the Catholic religion (and religion in general) would ever come under attack, as it reputedly does in some state universities. My main concern was the possibility of their falling in love and eventually marrying someone not of their faith. And I am old-fashioned enough to believe that mixed marriages are not the ideal—a conviction that is shared by most Protestants as well....Many of my students were from "mixed-religion" homes, and most of them had not been raised in the Catholic faith. As I remember, almost universally the students agreed that it is better for one of the parents to convert to the other's religion so that one faith would prevail in the home; and that was all right with me as long as it was the Catholic religion that was to be adopted by both parties. Ecumenical as I am, I could not feel

comfortable in agreeing with a couple of my best Catholic students when they considered converting to the Lutheran Church. So I had to search my own heart: maybe I was not very ecumenical at all.[73]

The question distressed him so much in the mid-1970s, that he discussed it with some of his Luther College colleagues and also with a dear friend of longstanding, a convert to Catholicism. The old friend reassured him that, "students are going to have to live in a society that includes all faiths and mixed marriages often work out. If your Catholic students are given some pride in being Catholics, if they grow in their faith, then by being in a Lutheran college they may come out better Catholics."[74] Apparently, that was enough to allow the matter to be laid to rest in his mind.

One Luther student who was particularly influenced by Fr. Emeric Lawrence's presence on campus was John Dietzenbach '74, a Roman Catholic native of Fort Atkinson, Iowa. Dietzenbach was drawn to Luther both because of its fine educational reputation and because of the generous financial aid package awarded to him in 1970, as he began his studies. Though Dietzenbach never had Emeric for a teacher, he was among the active "Romans," the close-knit group of Catholic students to whom Emeric ministered as chaplain. Dietzenbach did not recall ever having a discernment discussion with Emeric about his vocation, but over the years, became profoundly moved by Emeric's obvious joy in the priesthood. He went on to seminary after graduation, and became a diocesan priest in Maryland. It is probably of Dietzenbach that Emeric wrote with great anticipation in his weekly Epistle to the Romans, "I hope I can live to see the day when the first Luther College alumnus or alumna becomes a priest..."[75]

Emeric Lawrence's approach to ecumenical living was by no means always serious. As Will Bunge noted in his article about Emeric:

> His parties during the Luther years were legendary, better experienced than described. They were a kind of ecumenical crossroads—an occasion for meeting others from the college, Decorah, St. John's, Emeric's family, and getting to know these diverse people as friends, as opportunities for enriching life.[76]

Fr. Emeric himself remarked in his Journals:

> Some of the best parties of my life have been the ones I've had for my Lutheran colleagues and their wives...Could it be that

> parties have been too much neglected as an instrument of ecumenism?[77]

Emeric's ecumenical efforts on the Luther campus also produced much humor, the mark of excellent relations. In his Journals, Emeric Lawrence remembered several examples:

> I received some interesting pieces of mail in those days. When I was at Concordia College, I received a letter addressed to "Fr. Luther Emeric." It was from [Business Manager] Erling Naeseth of Luther College. And I still have this card from a beauty shop downtown. It says, "We welcome you to Decorah. If you present this card to Jane (Shirley was crossed out), a free shampoo finger wave is waiting for you." That was addressed to "Mrs. Emeric Lawrence."
>
> At the end of my second year here [at Luther] when I had to leave, [English professor] Mary Lou Mohr had a dream—that I had been elected Pope. And ever since then I've had a great love for Mary Lou. Dream on, Mary Lou, but it's getting a bit late.
>
> I must tell you about an unfulfilled desire I've had for eight years—to organize a midnight candle-light procession to the statue of Martin Luther over there and recite the rosary. And I'm sure that Blessed Martin would know what it was all about.[78]

As far as anyone knows, Emeric never carried out his secret longing to pray in front of the statue of Martin Luther, but his great effectiveness as a Catholic ecumenist among Lutherans was enhanced by his obvious respect for "Blessed Martin." In the summer just before beginning the exchange, Emeric had read as much about Lutheran theology as he could get his hands on, including John Todd's *Life of Luther*.[79] On Christmas Day midway through the first year of the exchange, he noted in his Journal with an air of mock surprise, "I've been spending most of the day in bed nursing my cold...and reading. I happened to see Roland Bainton's biography of Luther in the room I am using, and before I knew it, I was engrossed. Imagine me reading a biography of Luther on Christmas Day! This is what one semester at Luther College has done to me!"[80]

Fr. Emeric's sympathy for Luther's critical stance against the Church went only just so far, however. Despite eight years of life at Lutheran institutions of higher learning and scores of deep friendships with good Lutherans, there remained limits to his endorsement of Luther's historical actions. As his ecumenical contacts at Luther College strengthened his commitment to Roman Catholicism, he began to feel in a new and deeper way the gap between the faith traditions and the drive toward reconciliation that had come to define his vocation in that place:

> No matter how friendly I felt towards Lutheran history, including Martin Luther himself, some of its traditional liturgical practices and above all towards "my" Lutheran colleges and my countless friends in both, I could never bring myself to agree that leaving Catholicism with all its treasures (yes, even its faults and failures) in terms of sacraments, liturgy, liturgical celebrations, history and prayer life for any other faith could be an enrichment. I hesitate and grieve to have to write this, and I pray that my Protestant friends will not write off our friendship because of my frankness....If ever the agony of separation and the consequent need for our coming together became more apparent to me it was in deciding to write this paragraph.[81]

In the end, his Lutheran friends, particularly those among the Religion faculty at Luther College, were instrumental in helping Emeric understand both his reaction to the historical Luther and their own ecumenical embrace of the priest-monk from St. John's University who had enlivened the Luther campus for so long. The Religion department chair Harris Kaasa replied to the above confession:

> I do not find what you say here in the least offensive. I don't think that anyone here ever imagined that you were (and are) anything but a devoted son of the Catholic Church. It is meet, right, and salutary that your primary loyalty should be to that Communion. It is even understandable that you should perforce feel that the Catholic Church has a kind of 'fulness' that is lacking elsewhere.[82]

During his time at Luther College, and also at Concordia, Emeric Lawrence himself was changed by his encounter with people, and the two educational institutions of the Protestant faith tradition. Dr. Harris Kaasa dubbed it "The Evolution of Emeric," between the time of his 1967 Journal and that of 1974–75.[83] At Kaasa's explicit request, Emeric wrote about the change in himself and his ecumenical work over the years that he had been in residence at Luther College. Fr. Emeric reflected thus in his Journals:

> It was evidently not a sudden or abrupt change of perspective. It came about gradually by means of familiar contacts with my students and above all with members of the Religion Departments of the two colleges [Luther and Concordia]. Naturally, I was also much influenced by the political and social climate of the national scene during those years and last but surely not least, by the people and clergy (Protestant and Catholic) of the two cities I lived in (Decorah and Moorhead)....[I]t is apparent to me that during my first two years with the Lutherans, my preoccupation was almost entirely ecumenical. I spoke in many Protestant churches and to Protestant groups of all denominations, and my sermons at St. Benedict's parish, Decorah, often extolled the ideal of Christian unity. Meanwhile, at Luther College a growing friendship developed with members of the administration and faculty and also with students.[84]

Despite his personal pain at the continued separation of the faith community at Luther College, and elsewhere in the world, Emeric eventually came to appreciate the special place that he had acquired at the college. He took great pride and delight in his unique function as a decidedly Roman Catholic monk among such strongly committed Protestants:

> Now they take me for granted, I said to myself several times during those years. Being taken for granted was a considerable change from the curious but reserved greeting I encountered when I first went to Luther in 1967. Being taken for granted there was good I hasten to add. It simply meant being accepted as a teacher, a frequent preacher in the daily chapel service and a regular member of the college faculty. It was something I had dimly hoped would come about, but hardly expected back in those pioneer days of the exchange program between Luther and St. John's University.[85]

One experience during the January Term of 1974 stands out as most significant in Emeric Lawrence's last years as a visitor to Luther College. In many ways, the experience represents the culmination of his work as an ecumenist at Luther. The January experience would also become a model for the kind of international study that has come to characterize Luther College. The January Term experience grew directly out of the Luther College-St. John's exchange of theologians. In his Journals, Fr. Emeric Lawrence, who co-led the course in January 1974, explained its evolution:

During his exchange year at St. John's Professor Joseph Everson of Luther College became a close friend of Father Preston Moss, a native Bahamian priest who was studying for his M.A. degree in theology at St. John's. Between them they came up with a possible project for a January term, open to students from Luther, St. John's and St. Benedict's colleges. The project involved the students helping with the teaching and other scholastic activities at Aquinas and St. Augustine's Schools in Nassau.[86]

During the second year, in which Fr. Emeric Lawrence was involved, the joint venture drew together fifteen students, thirteen from Luther and two from St. Benedict's College, the sister institution to St. John's. The Interim course was called "The Role of the Church in a Changing Society," and involved separate teaching assignments at the Stapledon School for the Mentally Retarded (three students), Aquinas College (seven students), and at St. Augustine's School (five students), which had been run for many years by the Benedictine monks of St. John's Abbey, Collegeville.

Under the leadership of Professor Everson and Father Zachary Williams, the 1973 experiment was so well received by the administration and students of the two schools that an invitation was extended for a similar project in January 1974. When Professor Everson asked me to be his co-leader for the group, I was delighted, since I had never been to the Bahamas, the scene of over seven decades of missionary labors by my St. John's *confreres*. January 1974 was to become one of the most memorable experiences of my Luther College career.[87]

For the first time, Luther College students were traveling together with Catholic students in order to experience teaching in another culture. While the ostensible focus was on teaching, it was clear that spontaneous ecumenical sharing would occur among the student teachers, the ecumenical faculty, and their young Bahamian charges and school personnel. The course promoted what Emeric Lawrence had long believed would eventually allow for Christian unity—lay people from both traditions in working contact with each other. With great satisfaction, Emeric noted in his Journals:

Our Luther students have all come to know and greatly admire some of the nuns, priests and brothers and the lay teachers. From an ecumenical point of view, I think this is terribly important. In my Christmas letter to relatives and friends I remarked how great it was that Luther students (and two from St. Benedict's [College] should spend three weeks (at their own expense all the way) teaching in Catholic schools. Now I am even more enthusiastic, having witnessed the experiment.[88]

On May 4, 1975, the fortieth anniversary of Fr. Emeric's ordination to the priesthood, he was honored by a special Mass at St. Benedict Church. Decorah area clergy of all denominations, the Luther

*Luther College Religious Department*

*Knights of Columbus*

College Religion faculty, the Knights of Columbus of St. Benedict's parish, the abbot from St. John's, and many other special friends marched in a procession to the Mass. At the reception in the church basement following the event, Luther College President E. D. Farwell and several others paid tribute to both Emeric, and the successful exchange between Luther and St. John's University. The *Decorah Journal* of May 8, 1974, reported, "Speakers at Sunday's program...attested to how well the exchange has worked out on both Lutheran and Catholic campuses in 'building bridges instead of walls...,' Dr. Farwell stated, 'We love this man' in referring to the popular Benedictine monk, while Father Emeric said, 'This has been the most marvelous experience of my life.'"[89] The parish gift collected at the occasion would normally have gone to Fr. Emeric himself, but, as the *Decorah Journal* also reported, the generous Emeric asked instead that it be given to a Luther student from Nigeria to allow him, his wife and their two children to return home to Africa following his graduation from Luther that spring.[90]

The anniversary event gave Fr. Emeric occasion to take stock of his contribution to the ecumenical movement and of the role of

Luther College and Decorah in his own personal growth because of the years he had spent in that place:

> Later, at the reception in the parish hall there were speeches by President Farwell, Bill Ronan (representative of St. Benedict's parish), my dear friend Harris Kaasa, and my equally dear friend Fr. White, former pastor of St. Benedict's with whom I lived and worked for five years...I guess I felt a bit humbled by it all—as though I had planned this anniversary celebration to give people an occasion to praise me. Of course, I do take considerable satisfaction in having breeched some walls and bridged some gaps, as Fr. White credited me with doing. But actually, I didn't have any such intentions when I first came or at any time during my years here (and at Concordia). I just tried to be myself both at the college and in the city, and apparently something good has happened. I think, too, that my passion for ecumenism, my pain at the divisions among Christians, has also come through to the community.
>
> But where or how does one distinguish between grace and human desire and effort? If God has used me, it is simply an additional reason for the gratitude to God that I have experienced these past few days....If I have been good for Luther College and for this community, they have also been good for me. So we are even. I can never be sufficiently grateful to Father Colman Barry and President Farwell for having initiated the professor exchange between St. John's and Luther College and to Abbot Baldwin for having allowed me to be the one who started (and apparently finished) it all off. It was a weekend I shall never forget.[91]

After eight years, the Luther College-St. John's University exchange of theologians came to an end. Following his time at Luther, Emeric Lawrence reflected on his extraordinary assignment to Luther College and on all of his experiences in a book-length manuscript he had hoped would be published in his lifetime. It was fittingly called "The Lutheran Journals of a Catholic Monk" and spanned the time between his arrival in Decorah in the fall of 1967, and the end of his work back at Luther in 1974. In the manuscript, which was never published, Emeric Lawrence concluded:

> So now the adventure is over, and I have entered upon a new and different vocation, that of a hospital chaplain. I think I am a different man than I was back in 1967 when it all began.

> I hope I am a better man, a better priest. One thing I am sure of is that the experience of living and associating with students and colleagues at these two Lutheran colleges [Luther College and Concordia College] on religious, intellectual and social levels has brought out qualities of self-confidence and self-awareness that I didn't know I had. Best of all, I think I have grown in my appreciation of people—people in general and members of other denominations than my own in particular.[92]

Much later, Fr. Emeric Lawrence reflected back on the benefits that had come from the years at Luther College and also Concordia College, for himself as well as for the state of ecumenical understanding in this small part of the world:

> I am convinced that the whole experience [at Luther College] was providential. Simply because I felt challenged and felt that I represented the Catholic Church, I forced myself to study, and I think I grew in knowledge and understanding, and I hope, in wisdom, to a degree that might not have happened if I had remained in an exclusively Catholic atmosphere like St. John's.
>
> I might indulge in a certain (and I hope, justified) vanity in believing that because of my presence on these campuses, the Roman Catholic Church is more respected in those parts of the country. And what, in the end, is more necessary for the eventual coming together of our Churches than mutual understanding and respect?[93]

Fr. Emeric Lawrence had had an extraordinary effect on the Luther College campus, chiefly because of his person and his innate ability to undertake successfully the delicate work of bridge building. Bruce Wrightsman of the Luther College Religion faculty remarked in a tribute:

> I will close with one last point—[Emeric's] reconciliation of many potential contentious factions on this campus. . . Faculty and Administration, Senior Faculty and Junior Faculty, Students and Faculty, Students and Administration, and within our Religion department, between those of us who are conservative and those of us who are liberal or even radical in our theology. He transcended all of these divisions, not because he was an outsider—for he is not—but he overcame them by simple good will and love. And in the process, he showed us what we all know but often forget; the power of God's love to heal any kind of separation, to reduce any human barrier.[94]

In eight years of pioneering work, the Catholic monk-priest from St. John's University had helped to open Luther College to considerable ecumenical outreach. Doubting and questioning were very much a part of the process, but so were humor and care for others. Fr. Emeric Lawrence had certainly not done it alone, nor had it happened in a vacuum. The extraordinary ecumenical exchange between Luther College and St. John's had occurred because there were extraordinary people on both campuses who made a commitment to further ecumenism.

In the weeks just before Fr. Emeric Lawrence had embarked on the first leg of his journey to Luther College some eight years earlier, he had written in a letter:

> We are so close together, and yet so far apart. As Hans Küng says, "we must rejoice over that which unites us—despite all differences—it is more than that which separates us...." Many things Luther praised are no longer restricted to the Protestant Church nor are those things he censured to be found exclusively in the Catholic Church. Neither Catholics nor Protestants can consider themselves exempt from making a continuous effort to model themselves upon the apostolic Church.[95]

In the time of his residence at Luther College, Fr. Emeric rejoiced over that which united Catholic and Protestant. In both word and example, he continually reminded the Christians he encountered of the challenging mandate to be one. In the last months of his tenure at Luther, Fr. Emeric wrote of an extraordinary encounter with that oneness, in its all too often broken form. He encountered that oneness at Luther College, during a service to mark the beginning of Lent for Christians worldwide. The words recall his experience eight years earlier, the painful separation between Lutherans and Catholics in the Eucharist that he experienced first hand at Luther during the first Mass ever celebrated on the campus. In the intervening years, Fr. Emeric Lawrence had helped the college community come much closer to unity, yet still felt the wide gap between the faith traditions. Emeric's journal entry for the ordinary class day of Thursday, February 13, 1975, is offered here in its entirety. It represents the best of Emeric Lawrence, Luther College ecumenist extraordinaire:

> Today is the day after Ash Wednesday, my last Ash Wednesday at Luther College. I am sure it will be one that I will remember as long as I live. I had my own two Masses, of course, one at the parish and one at the college for the Romans. Then

I had another Ashes service in late afternoon at the college, helped Fr. Lechtenberg impose ashes at his two evening Masses and then went up to the college chapel for the Service of the Ashes there.

It was the third such service we have had at the college and easily the most memorable. I recall the theme of the first one in 1973 when the young intern pastor from Yale (I think) suggested the idea of a Catholic blessing and imposing of ashes. The theme that first Ash Wednesday was that of the Phoenix, the mythical bird that consumes itself in fire and then rises triumphantly to a renewed life from its own ashes. The Christian inference is easy to make. We too die to the past life but only to rise with Jesus at Easter; and I suppose other inferences could be made as well.

Last night the theme was atonement; Pastor Smedsrud having got the idea (and the format of the service) from the Catholic magazine *Liturgy*, which in turn had been inspired by the Anglican priest who writes for *Worship*, Reginald Fuller. He suggested that we Catholics make Ash Wednesday a day of Atonement, a Christian Yom Kippur.

So we began with Pastor Smedsrud carrying into the darkened chapel a brazier with burning shavings. Pastor Refsal and I stood beside the brazier on its stand feeding the flame with branches of last year's palms, while Pastor Smedsrud read from Psalm 51, the Miserere, the universal act of contrition out of the heart of sinful mankind.

When we had burned all our old palms, I blessed the ashes and we imposed them on the foreheads of all who came forward. Then we read one of John the Baptist's exhortations to penance from the Gospel of Matthew, and I followed with a sermon on atonement, at-one-ment, reconciliation. I reminded them all of the beginnings of universal alienation as described in the creation story of Genesis with the disobedience of Adam and Eve. As a result of their failure to keep in mind their relationship to God, to one another, to nature and to their very own selves, alienation and disruption set in for all mankind and the only one capable of effecting at-one-ment is Jesus himself. But he can bring at-one-ment-only if we recognize our need for it, recognize our sad and sorry condition of estrangement. We've got to decide to pick ourselves up like the

> prodigal son and return to our Father, who is willing to forgive us unconditionally, no matter what we may have been or done.
>
> When the sermon was over, I suggested that we give one another a sign of reconciliation then and there; and I gave my two fellow chaplains the old monastic sign of peace, a kind of *embrazo* including contact between cheeks. I told the students to do what they wished, and almost all of them chose the same embrace we demonstrated.
>
> With the end of the service of ashes and atonement, I left the altar, and the other two continued with the Holy Communion service. I suppose I have never before felt the anguish and agony of our division into denominations so vividly. Here I had just spoken about reconciliation, we had demonstrated our feelings for one another and our desire for at-one-ment in a very dramatic manner, and I had to leave the very act of reconciliation, the Eucharist, to return to my office. Perhaps it is incorrect to say that I had to leave; but I would have felt out of place sitting on the side while the two of them stood at the altar. The gesture of my leaving must have been obvious to the students and members of the faculty present. But what they could not know or even guess was the pain I felt. However, I think that Pastors Smedsrud and Refsal knew...and the Lord too. May He soon end all our divisions![96]

Although even in its final days, the exchange with St. John's still engendered considerable enthusiasm on both campuses in theory, in practice it had become increasingly difficult for both the institutions to staff the endeavor any longer. For all practical purposes, Luther College had exhausted its small pool of young theologians able, with their families, to relocate to Collegeville for an entire academic year. And at St John's, there was the pressure to fulfill all of the Abbey's commitments to Minnesota churches and chaplaincy placements. At the conclusion of the 1974–75 academic year, Fr. Emeric Lawrence took up his new assignment as chaplain to the women of Saint Scholastica Monastery, Duluth. The decision to terminate the exchange was a difficult one for the Farwell administration that had so enthusiastically helped to give it birth eight years earlier. It was time to move on, both for the administration, and for the issue of ecumenicity.

In its eight years of existence, the exchange between St. John's University and Luther College had done remarkable work on both campuses and had sparked a pioneering ecumenical spirit in the Decorah community as well. Even as the exchange ended, it continued to produce fruit in the town of Decorah and at the college. The ongoing and very cordial working relationship between Luther College and St. Benedict Catholic Church was one such fruit, and ecumenical cooperation between the St. Benedict and the Lutheran churches of the town was another. A new ecumenical friendship between a local Catholic priest and a Lutheran pastor grew up in the aftermath. Fr. Edward Lechtenberg, senior pastor of St. Benedict Church (1975–1987) and Rev. Paul Christianson, senior pastor of First Lutheran Church (1972–1987) became fast friends and continued, both personally and with their congregations, the cooperation that Emeric Lawrence and others had helped to begin a decade earlier.

A very visible result of this new ecumenical collaboration was the Ulster Project, which ran from 1987–2000. The Project was initiated by Lechtenberg and Christianson, and annually brought to Decorah approximately ten teenagers from troubled Northern Ireland.[97] They were paired with young Catholic and Protestant hosts in Decorah, attended each others' church services, and learned about conflict resolution, together with their American counterparts and counselors of both countries. In support of the Ulster Project, the annual Irish Celebration, which for some twenty years had been held on St. Patrick's Day between the parishioners of St. Benedict's and the congregation of First Lutheran Church, became the annual Ulster Stew Supper, held every March.

Further evidence of the extraordinary ecumenical cooperation in Decorah that grew out of the exchange was the long running Decorah Ministerium, a monthly gathering of all Christian clergy for bible study and fellowship. In 2002, the Ministerium became the Interfaith Coalition which hosts a Community Food Pantry and a Free Medical Clinic, both housed at First Lutheran Church and staffed by volunteers from area churches. Local congregations also share responsibility for staffing the Depot Outlet, Meals on Wheels, and entertainment and board membership for a local nursing home.

## Subversive Ecumenism

**Wilfred F. Bunge**
Professor Emeritus of Religion and Classics
B.A. Luther College; M.A, University of Iowa; B.Th. Luther Theological Seminary; Th.D. Harvard University

*Wilfred Bunge was the first exchangee in Religion from Luther College to St. John's University in 1967. Now retired with grace, he maintains a strong and welcome presence on the Luther campus and recently authored "Who We Are: A Brief History of Luther College"*

The pace of social change over the past forty years has been such that one has to struggle to recall what the relationship between Lutherans and Roman Catholics was like prior to the 1960s. The calling of the Second Vatican Council by Pope John XXIII was a watershed event whose consequences were more dramatic than anyone at the time could have imagined. Conceived as a thorough examination of Catholic thought and practice with a view toward giving that thought and practice a genuinely twentieth century expression, it opened the door to social changes that went far beyond the intentions of its designers.

The documents that resulted from the theological discussions of the Vatican II Council, often with participation by Protestant guest theologians, were not in themselves radical departures from tradition. The title "separated brethren," assigned to non-Catholic churches, was something less than total recognition of their legitimacy, implying an eventual return to the one church centered in Rome. Nonetheless, the simple fact of openness to positive relationships among churches signaled the promise of an end to almost 450 years of stand-offish and even hostile relationships.

Until the 1960s it had been possible to maintain a high degree of social separation between Roman Catholics and members of other churches. For example, both sides discouraged intermarriage; this did not mean that such intermarriage never occurred. However, especially in rural communities, social sanctions tended to keep the numbers down. Since, on the whole, Catholic priests exercised stronger control over the religious behavior of their members than Protestant clergy, mixed marriages more often than not resulted in the Protestant spouse transferring to the Catholic fold. Short of this, at least the children grew up Catholic.

There were undoubtedly multiple social factors that broke down barriers between members of different religious groups in the mid-twentieth century. The changes introduced by Vatican II were not the only motivation. In fact, Vatican II may in part have resulted from changes in the larger social world. Updating, or *aggiornamento*, which became the slogan of the Vatican II Council, directly states the connection between changes in the church and changes that had already occurred in the general socio-cultural world. These changes were exerting pressure on the church to adapt. People were no longer experiencing differences in religious traditions as a major social barrier to intimate relationships, particularly marriage, that most intimate of human relationships. Take, for example, the current rate of intermarriage between Jewish people and non-Jews. This rate has increased gradually over the past several decades, until it has reached a level of almost 50% of all marriages in which one of the partners is Jewish, a situation viewed as a major threat to the future of a distinctively Jewish identity. One could argue that this indicates a significant decrease in the importance of religious traditions to their members. That is, religion plays a smaller role in self-identity than it has in the past. On the other hand, one could also argue that this situation grows out of the breakdown in the social isolation of religious communities in the twentieth century. All sorts of differences—for example, differences in cultural and ethnic background, in socioeconomic status, in "race," as well as in religious loyalties—no longer loom so large as they once did in such intimate choices as marriage.

These social factors were in part the motivation for the project of *aggiornamento* in Pope John XXIII's call for an ecumenical council. The Council was to deal with these factors and others in bringing the expression of the church up to date. In a strange way, however, the attention to *aggiornamento* gave a kind of permission for Catholic Christians and others to initiate their own social updating entirely apart from the authorization of theologians. Intermarriage between Catholics and non-Catholics is but one example of this. Another example from Catholic moral theology is the virtual abandonment of traditional birth control practice among lay Catholics. The major changes that were occurring at the same time with respect to the role of women, that is, the entry of women into a wide variety of occupations that had previously been largely restricted to men, were a part of the twentieth century. When the church proposes a project of *aggiornamento*, it must of necessity confront that aspect of contemporary life that has to do with the changing role of women in society.

The vocation of pastor or priest, which is in any case problematic in an increasingly self-indulgent social world, becomes especially problematic when it involves vows of poverty, obedience, and celibacy. Thus it should have been apparent that "updating" would reduce the appeal of the special vocations to the priesthood and monastic life. This would have happened to some degree even if Vatican II had never occurred. However, the ecumenical council, called for the express purpose of *aggiornamento*, arguably encouraged the development toward the crisis in such vocations since Vatican II.

Such developments constitute what I have termed subversive ecumenism. The traditional social barriers formed by differences in religious loyalties break down once those differences are no longer so pronounced. Religious differences decline in importance when people make decisions concerning such things as education and marriage. Catholics, who were once socialized primarily in elementary, secondary, and even higher education institutions of the church, now freely choose to attend public schools or higher education institutions identified with other churches. Religious differences decline in importance, and people make such choices as marriage without major concern for those differences.

Ironically, the emergence of "diversity" as a positive goal for institutions and communities toward the end of the twentieth century may be due in large part to the diminution in the importance of differences. Once those differences have declined in importance, their vestigial remains are promoted and celebrated as signs of the health of communities. What were once viewed as barriers to intimate relationships, we now actively seek out and promote as enrichments of those relationships. The end result, of course, will be the further erosion of said differences, and a rapidly increased rate of socio-cultural homogenization. Pockets of resistance and repristination will surely develop, and everyone will admire their quaintness and charm. However, these will be minority communities, something like the Amish. After all, who does not marvel at the sight of buggies and old-fashioned lifestyles from the comfort of super modern automobiles as we speed by? The vast majority will enjoy a new form of homogeneity.

As we pioneered the professorial exchange between St. John's University in Collegeville, Minnesota, and Luther College in 1967, we were in the midst of the changes described above. Thus they were not in the forefront of our thinking. We considered ourselves pioneers in a bold new experiment, not realizing that we were actually being carried along on a larger social current to which we had made only a very small contribution. Perhaps we can claim no more than that we implicitly recognized changes that were occurring. We gave them public notice.

When President Farwell invited me to be the first Luther College faculty member to participate in the faculty exchange with St. John's, I had had very little experience with Roman Catholics, and Roman Catholic theology. Thus, it was with some nervousness that my wife Ruth and I visited St. John's in the late spring of 1967 to make arrangements for the yearlong stay. We met with Father Colman Barry, then president of St. John's, in his office. He had invited one of St. John's faculty members in economics to join us for the evening. Father Emeric Lawrence was also there. Father Colman had his radio turned to KSJR, the station that recently had had its beginning at St. John's, the station that was the beginning of Minnesota Public Radio. It was obviously one of his favorite ventures, and he clearly had an ear fixed on the station throughout our conversation. He complained at one point that the station was not including enough news about the church, and that he had registered his unhappiness over this with Bill Kling, a graduate of St. John's, whom Father Colman had appointed to get the project started.

That night we were guests in one of the guest rooms of the Abbey, a very comfortable room except that it was very overheated. We had opened a window to bring down the temperature. I recall that the drapes were fluttering from the breeze this created. In my dreams I somehow connected these fluttering drapes with the habits of nuns, who were hovering menacingly over us. A strange dream, in view of the innocent and non-threatening image of nuns today in popular advertising. However, the dream probably arose out of my subconscious uneasiness about things Catholic.

There still existed, though perhaps in its declining stages, that special Roman Catholic ethos of church schools. Where nuns, who brooked no nonsense, were in charge. This experience instilled a culture of religious piety, which those of us on the outside recognized as a very distinctive and complex culture quite different from our own. Obligatory Mass attendance once a week, the confessional, the rosary prayer beads, crossing oneself, holy water, genuflection, due respect for the saints and the Blessed Virgin—the whole lot constituted a world of which we were mere observers. Acquaintances who grew up in this culture still evoke it as a formative experience of their childhood years. Interestingly, however, they speak of it with a combination of dismissiveness and nostalgia, as of a somewhat oppressive world that once existed but no longer does, a quaint world whose charm improves with distance.

We thoroughly enjoyed our year at St. John's, made many friends and were welcomed with typically openhearted Benedictine hospitality. Since St. John's is a project of a Benedictine Abbey, the distinction between lay faculty and faculty who were members of the order is a prominent feature of the University. This was new to my experience. The governance of the institution seemed more hierarchical than anything I had heretofore experienced. I got the impression that decisions made at faculty meetings might be vetoed or altered at a subsequent meeting of the monastic chapter. Though I cannot cite a particular instance of this, the very impression that it could occur exercised an influence on the corporate life of the community.

In the course of the year, and subsequently, it became clear to me why the saying of Mass was so central to Father Emeric's concerns as he faced the prospect of the faculty exchange. The Mass is central to the Catholic ethos in a way that has not been true of the Eucharist in Protestant practice. The magnificent Abbey Church at St. John's was the chief gathering place for the entire university community. The opening convocation of the academic year occurred there, and it was the venue for commencement exercises at the conclusion of the year. On both occasions, Mass was central to the event.

Thus it came as no surprise on my return to Luther the following year to discover that Emeric did in fact say Mass on campus, and he issued an open invitation to attend. Attend we did, in large numbers, and we participated in the Mass along with Roman Catholic students and Emeric's special Roman Catholic friends from the Decorah community. It was wonderful. Emeric had just the right personality to make everyone feel at ease and welcome at the central rite of Roman Catholic worship. I had not in fact participated in the Mass during the year at St. John's, though I occasionally attended Catholic worship services. I did not want to break protocol, so to speak. This hesitation disappeared, however, when I got to know Emeric better the following year, his second year at Luther as a participant in the exchange.

It occurs to me that the Eucharist is the central rite of hospitality in the Christian tradition. This should come as no surprise, since sharing a meal together is probably the most common way in which we form relationships with others, welcome them and acknowledge their importance. Nowhere is this better observed liturgically than in the Catholic Church. Thus any attempt at improved relationships among Christians comes inevitably to the question whether we welcome each other to our Eucharist. Though officially the churches tend to follow the principle that theological agreement precedes Eucharistic fellowship, I have come to doubt the wisdom of that sequence. Thus I recommend active subversive ecumenism with respect to Eucharistic fellowship. Just do it, and theological discussion will follow. This too is a form of *aggiornamento*, active subversion added to the passive subversion of social change.

A new form of *aggiornamento* has overtaken the deliberate theological *aggiornamento* of Vatican II. This is the sociological *aggiornamento* that operates in all social situations throughout human experience, but now happens at a pace unprecedented in human experience. Pope John XXIII, when he called the Vatican II Council, undoubtedly recognized that this new tempo of social change required urgent theological reflection. Ironically, however, the results of that reflection both adapted to change and speeded it at the same time, especially as concerns interactions among religious communities.

The excitement in the church in the 1960s was the new opening in the Catholic Church to other churches. After centuries of separation and even hostility, it was refreshing to look forward to what might come of the new openness to dialogue and shared experience. It was a hopeful time, a challenging time, and a time for reexamination of longstanding positions and attitudes, with the possibility of change. Since then the concord between Lutheran and Roman Catholics on the doctrine of justification by faith has been the most significant theological development. Other theological agreements may in time follow. In the meantime let us share our common meal together in the confidence that the Lord Jesus Christ is our host and that He practices open communion.

Chapter Three

# H. George Anderson as President and Bishop

A new chapter in the ecumenical life of Luther College began when H. George Anderson assumed the presidency in January 1982.[98] Among the first things Anderson noticed was the relatively thin Catholic presence on the campus. By that time, the population of Catholic students had grown to about 200, but the pastoral and sacramental offerings to them on the campus diminished significantly since the end of the exchange with St. John's University and the departure of Fr. Emeric, seven years earlier.

In the heyday of the exchange, the "Catholic Life and Thought" course had been offered every semester. Catholic students were able to attend not only a special campus Mass on Sundays, but often several times during the weekdays as well. In notes and messages to Catholic students, Emeric regularly reminded them that he was available to them "day or night" for whatever they needed from him in pastoral care. In addition, each Catholic student at Luther College received a lengthy newsletter every week, written by Emeric just for them and posted to their student mailboxes, regardless of whether they attended the Masses or not.

Following Emeric's departure, however, the "Catholic Life and Thought" course had been reduced to one offering per year, the Mass on campus to once a month, and the newsletter had disappeared entirely. The pastoral care of the growing Catholic student body on campus now fell to the young associate pastors assigned to St. Benedict Church in Decorah, only one of their many duties in the large parish. The associates, in rapid succession, Frs. James Secora, Russell

Meyerhofer, and John Paisley, had been trained to function primarily as parish pastors and were naturally not as grounded in the academic world as Frs. Emeric, Durken, Williams, and Theisen had been.

Almost immediately, President Anderson took steps to strengthen the Catholic presence on campus, and, in 1983, directed the new campus pastor, Karen Bockelman, to take some initiatives in that regard. Bockelman established contact with the Roman Catholic Archbishop of Dubuque, Daniel Kucera, in whose diocese Decorah is located. Bockelman and Kucera immediately liked each other and formed a good working relationship. In 1986, and again in 1991, Archbishop Kucera visited Luther College in order to co-preside with Bockelman in an ecumenical prayer service in the Main Hall of the Center for Faith and Life. They used the new *Lutheran-Roman Catholic Service of the Word*, which had been developed for early ecumenical encounters between Catholics and Lutherans in the United States.[99]

Designed to bring the two traditions together during the ecumenical thaw following Vatican II, the Service squarely confronted the historical situation underlying the nearly 400 year separation between them. It contained several prayers of reconciliation, including a penitential rite, in which the two faith traditions begged forgiveness from God. Catholic participants recited together, "...we beg forgiveness from you, O God of mercies, and from our Lutheran brothers and sisters, for all prejudices, offensive words, reproaches without foundation, reprehensible gestures, or sheer indifference oftentimes, by which we, or our forebears, have offended them...."

The Lutheran participants countered with a matching confession directed to their Catholic sisters and brothers, "...and we, in turn, also beg forgiveness from you, O God of mercies, and from our Catholic brothers and sisters...."The special event drew a large number of Lutherans and Catholics from the community, the college, and the whole region. The presence of the Archbishop in his elaborate regalia on the Lutheran college campus was especially important, both because of the progress being made on the Catholic-Lutheran dialogue at that time, and because it represented further witness to the already long history of ecumenical cooperation on the Luther College campus. The Service concluded with the prayer: Lord, hear the prayers of your people and bring the hearts of believers together in your praise and in common sorrow for their sins. Heal all divisions among Christians that we may rejoice in the perfect unity of your Church and move together as one to eternal life in your kingdom....

The first time that Lutherans and Catholics had worshiped together on the Luther College campus had been in the spring of 1968 at the gathering for Ash Wednesday described in such detail by Fr. Emeric Lawrence in an earlier chapter. But this event was the first time that an official representative of the Catholic hierarchy had joined them. The recognition stemming from the Archbishop's presence in 1983 conveyed the new message that ecumenical cooperation best involved more than just local cooperation, and changed the face of ecumenism at Luther College and beyond.

Early in his administration, Anderson stepped up his own involvement in the international arena and, almost by default, the college became acquainted with ecumenical work at the global level. In 1984, his second year in the Luther College presidency, Anderson was appointed to the Commission on Studies of the Lutheran World Federation, which focused on theological studies, ecumenical dialogue, and discussions of theological issues. Since the Commission followed a tradition of rotating its spring meeting place, Anderson used the occasion of the 125th anniversary of Luther College, to invite the Commission to meet on the Decorah campus for its weeklong business

*LWF Commission on Studies at Luther College, 1986*

meeting. The visit gave the commission members a chance to see the college, the area, and also to meet Luther students, faculty, and staff, as well as other people from the region.[100]

The business meeting itself was held for four days in the Recital Hall of the Center for Faith and Life on the Luther College campus. The entire proceedings were simultaneously translated into German, due to the presence of two delegates from the German Democratic Republic, who were characteristically fluent in Russian, but knew no English. Other participants came from Brazil, Argentina, Finland, South Africa, Norway, West Germany, Taiwan, Denmark, Sweden, Canada, and Hungary. Two professional translators and their professional equipment were sent to Decorah from the Lutheran World Federation headquarters in Geneva, Switzerland.

Proceedings were generally closed to the public, but under special arrangements, intermediate and advanced students of the Luther College German program were invited to attend selected portions of the deliberations in order to have exposure to German speakers at work and to experience the phenomenon of simultaneous translation. The experience opened a whole new world to the use, and challenges of language learning.

On the meeting agenda was the ecumenical question about how Lutherans ought to conduct themselves in the worship service of another denomination. With the ecumenical thaw had come more open encounters and visits to other churches; accordingly, the LWF had been asked to formulate guidelines, and the commission was charged with offering recommendations for its approval What was taken up that day on the stage of the CFL Recital Hall was not a monumental piece like the *Joint Declaration*, but rather, one of the series of rather mundane, but necessary details that also propels the movement toward Christian unity. Interestingly, it involved a practical issue of ecumenical living, like so many other daily concerns in the place where it was decided.

Attention to daily concerns continued in a different way at the conclusion of the gathering, as the delegates spread out through the area around and beyond the Decorah community. On the Saturday following the official meeting, delegation members were led to the small neighboring town of Postville, to the Good Samaritan Home, where they met with the director and some residents. They visited a farm where they saw the daily operations, and talked with local residents. On Sunday, each delegate was a guest of a different Lutheran congregation in the area; they either gave a simple official greeting from their country and the Lutheran World Federation, or served as the guest preacher for the day.

President Anderson was appointed as the Lutheran co-chair of the Lutheran-Catholic Dialogue in 1979.[101] By the mid-1980s, the Lutheran-Catholic dialogue had completed its work on Round VII and published its final report in 1985. The very next year, the German commission completed its work on Justification as well, and published it as *Lehrverurteilungen—kirchentrennend?*[102] The congruence of the two major studies—the American and the German—now appeared to make possible a major international convergence of opinion, on the issue of Justification. The Lutheran World Federation proceeded with a proposal to test a joint declaration among its then 123 member churches throughout the world.

While the proposal stemming from Round VII made its way through international ecumenical channels, Anderson continued his work as Luther College president and, simultaneously, as the Lutheran co-chair of Round VIII, on the role of Mary and the saints. Round VIII completed its work in 1990 and published its final report, *One Mediator, Mary and the Saints*, in 1992.[103]

By the end of Round VIII, however, Anderson's unique challenge of chairing a national ecumenical dialogue team and also running a college had become unwieldy, even for someone so proficient at negotiating between tasks. In 1992, Anderson asked to be replaced on the dialogues, since meetings of the dialogue now regularly conflicted with traditional events at the college for which the president was expected to be present. There was nothing to be done; all efforts to establish a different timetable for dialogue meetings had failed because of the equally difficult schedules of the other dialogue members. On April 25, 1990, Anderson wrote to his Catholic co-chair, J. Francis Stafford, Archbishop of Denver:

> At its most recent meeting the ELCA's Standing Committee on Ecumenical Affairs received notice of my resignation as the Lutheran co-chair. I wanted you to know of this directly from me...I want you to know how grateful I am for the experience of working with the Catholic team on this project. It has been a unique window on Catholic thought, but, more significantly, a life-shaping opportunity to experience the unity of the Spirit in the bond of peace. I have learned a lot from you, and my only regret is that I will be losing that opportunity in the future...[104]

Anderson's resignation was accepted with pronounced reluctance on the part of those who had worked with him on the dialogue teams, both Lutherans and Catholics. The eminent Catholic theologian Avery Dulles, S.J., of Fordham University wrote, "I am extremely sorry that you will find it necessary to leave the dialogue, since your co-chairmanship has met with universal satisfaction...."[105] Anderson's Catholic co-chair of the Dialogue, J. Francis Stafford, Archbishop of Denver, wrote, "I know that Luther College is blessed to have you as its president. I will miss you and the keen insight and diplomatic strength which you bring to our discussions. I have grown over the years in my respect and admiration for you. Our semi-annual gatherings will certainly not be the same without you."[106] Sentiment among Lutheran members of the Dialogue was equally strong that,

> ...one would be remiss not to say thanks for the years of service and to salute the achievements in a difficult arena for which there are no textbook or preparatory courses....You entered into the tasks with a graciousness, reserve, proper gregariousness, and willingness to contribute that proved immensely helpful to all of us, on both sides, in the dialogue....[107]

Anderson was replaced as the Lutheran co-chair by Bishop Harold Skillrud of the Southeastern Synod.

That same year, partially in tribute to Anderson's work on the Dialogue rounds, Ruth Kath and Fr. Gary Krapfl proposed an Ecumenical Lecture Series to be held annually on the Luther College campus. Anderson, who was very supportive of the proposal, contributed to its inauguration by issuing official invitations to invited speakers over the next several years. Many of them Anderson knew personally from his longtime ecumenical work.

The inaugural speaker, Brother Jeffrey Gros, F.S.C., Associate Director, Ecumenical and Interreligious Affairs of the National Conference of Catholic Bishops in Washington, D. C., arrived in an unexpected April blizzard. Accordingly, his audience was small, but deeply interested in the new proposal which would be signed as the *Joint Declaration on the*Colleen Corcoran and

*Doctrine of Justification*, but not until some six years later. Bro. Gros concluded his lecture that evening with these prophetic words:

> As we pray for God's will for the Church in the world, we realize that we have received great blessings in the modern ecumenical movement. We can celebrate the blessings we have experienced, as we work to help others in the Christian community, who have not yet come to understand these blessings, see what we have been given in Jesus Christ for the building up of the unity of the Church. We realize that many still carry fears about ecumenical progress. It is prayer, study, mutual understanding and ecumenical experience that will cast out these fears. It is only by the experience and practice of Christian love that our institutional inertia can be overcome. It is by careful education of our people that deeper commitments and understanding can develop. We are grateful for the gifts of the Holy Spirit, and we pray for even deeper commitments on the part of our people to God's grace of unity.[108]

Ecumenical Lectures have been held annually since then at Luther College. Some have said that they might more accurately be named Interfaith lectures, since they have also brought to campus representatives from many faith traditions including Prof. William Chittick on Islam (1994), Prof. Jay Holstein on Judaism (1995) and Prof. Donald Luck on Buddhism (2001). In a unique tribute to Luther College's longtime connection to the country of Malta, the Ecumenical lecturer in 2005 was the noted Maltese priest and professor, Fr. Joseph Ellul, O.P., who addressed the Islam-Christian dialogue.

Over the years, inter-Christian concerns, particularly the Catholic-Lutheran dialogue as it has unfolded, has also received a substantial focus. In 1997, as part of the series Anderson, who was at that time

ELCA Presiding Bishop, was invited back to the campus, together with Archbishop Oscar H. Lipscomb of Mobile, Alabama, to discuss the *Joint Declaration*, which was still in proposal stage. Lipscomb had also been a member of the Lutheran-Roman Catholic dialogue, though at a separate time. During the visit they offered their perspectives on the proposal's strengths and weaknesses. The combination of the issue itself, and the presence of the beloved Anderson filled the Main Hall of the CFL almost to capacity. Among those in the audience were Archbishop Jerome Hanus, O.S.B., of Dubuque and Bishop Steven Ullestad, of the Northeast Iowa Synod of the ELCA.

Archbishop Oscar H. Lipscomb and Bishop H. George Anderson

In acknowledgment that it is sometimes the small personal encounters that most effectively deepen understanding between denominations, an ecumenical dinner had been held before the event for invited guests. Included were three Catholic students and their professor, Fr. Douglas O. Wathier, from Loras College in Dubuque. They were seated together with Luther students, professors, bishops, and clergy in ecumenically mixed tables. The evening was not without its own excitement, because of thick fog throughout the Midwest, Anderson still had not arrived as the dessert was being served, and nervous event organizers had begun to anticipate having to stage some sort of impromptu "Roman Catholic monologue" with Lipscomb. In the end, such plans proved unnecessary, as Anderson landed just in time.

At the well-attended public event that evening, the combination of gentle sparring and serious discussion between the two men gave the audience a small taste of the delicacy needed for the international negotiations. The proposal between the Lutheran World Federation and the Vatican would continue to be debated for another two years before the final agreement was reached. The event also showed Luther audiences a new side of former president Anderson, in his element as an ecumenical scholar and consummate consensus builder in the area of theology. It became clear that ecumenical negotiation was heavily dependent on persons like Anderson, who was both compassionate and forthright, as well as persistent and enormously patient with people and their ideas.[109]

As Anderson had moved from the Luther College presidency to the role of Presiding Bishop of the ELCA in 1995, the *Joint Declaration* proposal had continued its long and sometimes halting journey toward international ecumenical approval. A major step forward was achieved in August 1997, when ELCA Lutherans in the United States gave their resounding approval to the proposal at their biennial National Assembly. An ELCA news release reported immediately thereafter:

> Voting members at the Churchwide Assembly of the Evangelical Lutheran Church in America adopted by a vote of 958–25 a Joint Declaration on the Doctrine of Justification, declaring that condemnations the Lutherans hurled at Roman Catholics during the 16th century, concerning the key Lutheran doctrine of justification, no long apply to present Catholic teaching on this topic.[110]

Though a world-wide agreement on the *Joint Declaration* would take another two years and undergo numerous delays, Roman Catholics and Lutherans could take courage from the memory of that very special moment: Polling on the *Joint Declaration* had just been taken on the floor of the Assembly in Philadelphia. When the overwhelmingly positive vote was announced, there was a pause of stunned silence as the delegates suddenly realized what they had just done. Seconds later, they sprang to their feet clapping and cheering. Led by Anderson, the overjoyed assembly dissolved into singing the heartfelt doxology, "Praise God from Whom all Blessings Flow."[111]

Fittingly, a special invited guest at the 1997 ELCA Churchwide Assembly was Br. Jeffrey Gros, F.S,C., ecumenical spokesman for the National Conference of Catholic Bishops; as may be remembered, Gros had been the inaugural speaker for Luther College's Ecumenical Lecture series during the blizzard of 1993. Gros had addressed the voting members of the Assembly just days before the historic vote on the *Joint Declaration*, saying. "We broke off a conversation [about justification] at Regensburg, Germany, in 1541. Thirty years ago, shortly after Vatican II, we picked it up again...We have had nine rounds of dialogues with Lutherans since the 1960s. For the Roman Catholic Church, this agreement will be the first joint declaration ever to have been reached with any Reformation church since the 30-year process began."[112]

But the process of ratification still had a long road ahead; the Lutheran World Federation and the Vatican continued to refine the final agreement over the next two years:

> A Joint Declaration on the Doctrine of Justification was prepared by the Lutheran World Federation and the Pontifical Commission for Promoting Christian Unity in February 1995. After a preliminary circulation, the text was revised in June 1996 and again circulated. At the request of the LWF, some sections of this text were rewritten and a Final Proposal of the Joint Declaration was published in 1997....On June 16, 1998, following worldwide consultation of its member churches, the LWF Council unanimously approved the Joint Declaration.[113]

Some thirteen days after the positive Lutheran vote was announced, the Vatican responded with a resounding, "Yes, but..." Its major difficulties with the text—after Lutherans had voted to accept the draft—were widely scattered throughout the document and included sections on "the believer as simultaneously justified and sinner," and the "true ecclesial value" of the LWF's reception of the document, as well as some other areas.[114] Surprised and even stunned, many Lutheran negotiators reacted with disbelief. "[The Vatican response is] the worst news I've received during my whole career," said Harding Meyer of Germany, former director of the Ecumenical Research Institute of Strasbourg, France, and one of the drafters of the *Joint Declaration*.[115] Other equally distressed voices were raised in other corners of the globe.

However, ELCA Bishop Anderson, among the most seasoned negotiators in the dialogue, continued to listen beyond the reservations. Anderson said simply, "We have an agreement." Later he added, "Whatever differences remain, the document still contains a powerful statement of agreement on Christ's saving work."[116] In the end, the willingness to make that powerful statement of agreement prevailed, and following further high-level meetings, the Vatican announced in the fall of 1998 that the document, with a clarifying "Appendix" attached, was finally ready to be signed. A collective sign of relief was audible all over the world.

On October 31, 1999, in the city of Augsburg, Germany, the *Joint Declaration on the Doctrine of Justification* was signed in a masterfully arranged ceremony that began with an ecumenical vesper service the evening before in the Basilica of St. Ulrich and Afra. The ceremony continued with a Worship Service with Signing, that commenced in the Roman Catholic Cathedral and, following a ceremonial procession through the streets of Augsburg, concluded with the long awaited signing itself in the Lutheran St. Anna's Church.

The signatories were, for the Catholic Church, Edward Idris Cardinal Cassidy, President of the Pontifical Council for Promoting Christian Unity and Bishop Walter Kasper, Secretary of the Pontifical Council.[117] For the Lutheran World Federation, signatories were Bishop Christian Krause, President of the LWF, Reverend Dr. Ishmael Noko, General Secretary of the LWF, and LWF Vice-Presidents Dr. Sigrun Møgedal (Treasurer), Ms. Parmata Ishaya (Africa), Reverend Dr. Prasanna Kumari (Asia), and Bishop Julius Filo (Europe), Humberto Kirchheim (Latin America), and fittingly Bishop H. George Anderson (North America) was the last to sign. After Anderson had affixed his signature to both copies of the document, he closed the pen and put it down on the table with determination. The deed was finally accomplished, and via live-stream video and radio broadcasts, the historic moment was shared throughout the world.

At Luther College that same evening—halfway around the globe but very close in spirit to the Augsburg signing—a "Vespers Celebrat-

*Back row: Pastor Michael Blair, Heidi Torgerson, Chris Weber, Archbishop Jerome Hanus, Fr. Gary Krapfl. Front row: Pastor Joan Mau, Bishop April Ulring Larson, Mark Muggli, Carol Gilbertson, Ruth Kath.*

ing the *Joint Declaration*" was held in the Center for Faith and Life. Presiding together on the stage of the CFL were Bishop April Ulring Larson, ELCA (La Crosse, Wisconsin) and Jerome Hanus, O.S.B., Archbishop of the Dubuque Archdiocese (Dubuque, Iowa). Homilists for the evening were Professors Mark Z. Muggli and Carol Gilbertson, English professors at Luther College who have lived a purposefully ecumenical marriage for many years. The service was a fitting conclusion to a remarkable and historic day and a testimony to the pioneering ecumenical work that had been a part of Luther College for over thirty years.

Just two months later, in January 2000, an ecumenical study group joining Luther College and Loras College, stood in St. Peter's Square in Rome at midnight to usher in the new Millennium together. Together the Lutheran and Catholic students of the two colleges saw, and heard, Pope John Paul II proclaim from the papal window overhead, wishes to the world for a reign of peace in the new year. With a sea of 800,000 people, the event was televised throughout the world. After a week in Rome, the group journeyed to Wittenberg, Germany, the birthplace of the Reformation. They studied with intensity the newly-signed text of the *Joint Declaration on the Doctrine of Justification*. In the university where Luther taught, they wrote together in ecumenically mixed groups their own versions of the *Joint Declaration's* "Together we confess...." Later that same day, in the castle church, at the feet of Martin Luther's grave, the students lit a peace candle and prayed together, singing "Ubi Caritas" (Where There is Charity and Love). The group concluded the study tour at the Ecumenical Research Institute at Strasbourg, France; where they heard its director, Dr. Theodor Dieter, discuss the agreement just reached.

Reflecting back on the experience, one senior student was inspired to draw a parallel between the scientific research of her Biology major and other skills in critical thinking and foreign language that she had encountered during her studies at Luther College:

> I don't think I realized just how complex a process it is to define a common understanding between Lutherans and Catholics. The process they are going through is almost like a scientific method: They are trying to state all of the conditions (what Catholics and Lutherans believe) and controlling all of the variables by doing their best to avoid misunderstandings between groups due to a language barrier and changed meanings from

> translations. When working with such delicate issues of defining a church's faith, every word needs to be correct in its meaning and message. Translating the document for enough people to read in order to reach a consensus is an enormous task.[118]

A further enhancement of ecumenical visibility on the Luther College campus and beyond was made possible in 2002 by a five-year, $2 million grant from the Lilly Foundation Inc., designed to help students in the theological exploration of vocation. A particularly important and visible initiative that has taken hold at Luther is known as the "Vocation Visitor" program, which puts special emphasis on connecting students with alumni, church leaders, and other professionals with identifiable expertise. These are people who have given special thought to vocation and service, and who can show undergraduates the life and work of practitioners in the field. Under the auspices of the grant, Luther College has hosted many stimulating visitors, including President Emeritus—and now Bishop Emeritus—H. George Anderson. Anderson delivered the Opening Convocation Address for 2002–2003 on a "Sense of Vocation," and reminded the many first-year students present, "Your vocation is not just about you. It is about what you do with you. And what God can do with you..." Many of the more seasoned listeners in the group were reminded with those words just how much Anderson's own vocation to national and international ecumenical engagement had helped to move the whole Christian world closer toward understanding and acceptance.

Some months later, the campus would welcome another prominent international ecumenist under the Sense of Vocation program. Dr. Theodor Dieter, Director of the Ecumenical Research Institute in Strasbourg, France, came in early spring 2003 for a three-week residency in Decorah. The many classes, discussions, and conversations in which he participated at Luther during that time offered students, faculty, and staff another inside look at ecumenical engagement in action. The visits of two such committed international ecumenists to the Luther College campus added much to the worthy tradition of putting Luther students in direct contact with the larger church at work, quite fitting for this liberal arts college of the church, that for so many years has been following its vocation to ecumenical community building world-wide.

## Greeting

**April Ulring Larson**
Bishop, ELCA La Crosse Area Synod

Brothers and Sisters in Christ:

I bring you greetings from the Evangelical Lutheran Church in America on this wonderful celebration in conjunction with a celebration that happened earlier today in Augsburg, Germany, on the Joint Declaration on Justification. I am delighted to be standing here with Archbishop Hanus and I know that Bishop Anderson would love to be here. If we'd really been thinking we could have flown him from Augsburg because the signing actually happened about 3:00 this morning our time! It is wonderful for us to be gathered this evening among the goblins and the various roaming characters we saw as we came here this evening on this hallowed eve, October 31st.

This is a day when we do not discuss and defend the particularities of our church denominations. This is a day, rather, when we come together and celebrate our unity in Jesus Christ and our common understanding of this Joint Declaration on Justification. This is a day when we celebrate God bringing us closer and more visibly together as Christians. This is a day when we each can look at each other, face to face, and say how thankful we are for this God who has reached out to us through the incarnate presence of Jesus Christ, and this is a day when we can together look at this Jesus Christ and give thanks for a God who comes first to us and claims us as God's own.

Since Bishop Anderson could not be with us, but because he is dear to most of us as a former president of Luther College, as our present Presiding Bishop of our church, as a church historian and seminary president, I thought I would share with you some of his words regarding this statement which he himself worked on for almost two decades. He comments, in a statement on this Joint Declaration, that,

> ...in the last thirty years our relationship between the Roman Catholic Church and Lutheran Church has changed dramatically, chiefly as a result of the second Vatican Council. It has been possible for Lutheran and Roman Catholic theologians to sit down and discuss this whole area with a new perspective. First of all, there is great agreement today on how key Biblical passages are to be understood. Second, there is willingness to listen to the other side, to see where our traditional formulas may be understood or even to be one-sided. Finally, we have decoupled religion from politics sufficiently to discuss matters without having to assume that any concession will mean a loss of territory.

He also goes on to remind us that the United States had an agreement on justification in 1983, and much of that was helpful in the dialogue which produced this international joint declaration on justification. "What then does this all mean?" Anderson goes on to say. He spoke of having reached an important milestone and mentioned that there is still a road ahead, and he said, "I would elaborate a little on that image and say that we have reached a milestone situated as a sort of summit, maybe even a path, to the mountains." Differences still remain between our two traditions. Some of them are mentioned in the Joint Declaration itself. They must be addressed before the Christian unity that we have been praying for will come to pass. But this agreement on justification has added a key element to the cardinal points of belief that we already hold in common. It gives us one more assurance that we are reading from the same map, and that in God's providence we will one day walk together.

## Greeting

**Archbishop Jerome Hanus**, O.S.B.
Archbishop, Dubuque Archdiocese

It's a joy for me to be here. Thank you, Bishop Larson, for welcoming us Catholics to Luther College here in Decorah.

Geography is always important to Christian life, and Luther College symbolizes the journey that we have walked together for nearly forty years now. Luther College years ago entered into an ecumenical relationship with the Benedictines at St. John's in Collegeville. With joy as a Benedictine I come here to affirm and to stand humbly in that tradition.

Geography is important for us as Christians. Forty years ago when I began to study theology as a Roman Catholic, I thought there would be no better geographical location than Rome. So as a young twenty-three-year-old I headed to Rome. But I decided that I would make a stop on the way. I was traveling from northern Europe through Germany, to Switzerland, because one of my favorite authors at that time was a theologian by the name of Karl Barth. Barth was a great Calvinist, a Reformed theologian whose commentary on Romans in the first part of the century was a milestone in the making of theology. So I wanted to pay my respects to him.

While I was in Switzerland, where he was living at the time, I became aware of the fact that a young, unknown Catholic theologian had just finished his dissertation on Karl Barth's doctrine of the theology of justification. The conclusion of this scholarly German dissertation was that there wasn't much difference between Karl Barth and the Council of Trent. The name of that theologian was Hans Küng and this was his first book.

Karl Barth reportedly said if Küng's thesis is correct, I need to make a pilgrimage to Trent, that northern Italian city where the bishops of the Catholic Church gave such powerful force to the whole Catholic Reformation. In fact he did make a pilgrimage to Trent. Geography is important.

Today we not only gather here at Luther in Decorah, but our minds turn to Augsburg where that Joint Declaration was signed this morning. Augsburg and Wittenberg are so important to the history of Christian faith and Christian life. We stand in that long tradition of places where people have professed their faith, and now we stand together not only in Augsburg but here at Luther College.

Geography is important, and how could it be other than that when our Lord and Savior, the Incarnate Word of God, didn't just become incarnate in theory, but actually was born in Bethlehem and died and rose in Jerusalem for our salvation?

May we stand in praise to that great miracle of God's grace.

## Together We Confess

**Mark Z. Muggli and Carol Gilbertson**
Luther College

*Mark:* "We confess together that all persons depend *completely* on the saving grace of God for their salvation" (4.1).

*Carol:* "We confess together that *good works*, a Christian life lived in faith, hope and love, *follow* justification and are its fruits" (4.7).

*Mark:* And following that formula from the *Joint Declaration on the Doctrine of Justification*, we confess together our love for the *one church* of Jesus Christ, from which we draw our life.

*Carol:* We confess together our love for *distinct church traditions*, through which we believe the Spirit works.

All such declarations have beginnings. They begin with the Logos shaping the chaos into order, with God's redeeming transformation, through Jesus, of the unruly world. For us, these confessions have their roots in the particularity of the Dakotas on those vast, unconfining prairies that offer a liberating call to create things new.

*Mark:* I remember our darkened living room, with one single votive candle flickering beside a statue of Mary, which lived within an elaborate, wall-mounted wooden grotto hand-carved by a local monk. The rhythmical chant of my mother's leading the family Rosary tied us to the spin of eternity. I remember walking through the snow in the morning darkness to serve Mass for the local Benedictine Abbot. His liturgical clothes were more complicated than other priests', and he depended on us to hand him the right vestments in the right order; and these rituals ordered the whole world. I remember learning from the nuns and priests in my Catholic grade and high schools and from the nine first-cousins in my family, including my three brothers, who were Benedictine priests and nuns. I remember the year my father received the special honor as a Papal Knight of St. Gregory, and we were named the North Dakota Catholic Family of the Year by the Knights of Columbus.

*Carol:* I remember my mother's tales of her father, a Norwegian missionary casting out demons and healing lepers in Madagascar. I remember thinking it natural that my grandfather, my father, and all my eight uncles on both sides were Lutheran ministers and missionaries. I can still hear the fevered inflection of late-night adult talk at our Montana family cabin, about whether the Gospel was preached from one Lutheran pulpit or another. I remember my childhood awakening to the power of love's language in the weekly sermons at First Lutheran in Brookings, South Dakota. Each week my father mounted the pulpit, read the gospel, and ended with words from John, taken from the same chapter as our Gospel reading, "Sanctify us in your truth; your word is truth." Then he turned to us in the pew and smiled as he said, "Grace and peace to you, my dearest brothers and sisters, from our Lord and Savior, Jesus Christ." I remember a front-page newspaper photo of my parents and us six kids, heads bowed around the Thanksgiving table, a Protestant family praying table grace.

*Mark:* We confess together the power of education, and we thank God for the Spirit's presence in the Ecumenical and Reform movements of the twentieth century.

I remember St. John's University, a Benedictine college that was an early leader in Liturgical Reform and an important presence at the Second Vatican Council. I was the youngest of nine children who had attended St. John's and its sister college, St. Benedict. My first-year French teacher was Fr. Emeric Lawrence, who later became such a presence at Luther and in Decorah. My first Bible teacher there, in the mid-60s, was Wilfred Bunge, a Luther College faculty member who was part of the St. John's/Luther faculty exchange. He assigned the *Jerusalem Bible*, a newly completed Catholic translation. Prof. Bunge knew the Bible and had a keen Lutheran sense of the Fall, Sin, and Grace, but I'm fascinated that no one including my parents ever questioned that my first Bible course at our family's historic Catholic college was taught by a Lutheran. I recall my sadness at learning that the thin, slightly stooped man who joined us for Daily Mass at St. John's never received the Eucharist, because he was a Lutheran pastor and another of the Luther College professors; it was only thirty years later that I learned Leigh Jordahl's name. It was during these years that my father with his eighth-grade education struggled nightly through the thick published proceedings of Vatican II and my mother quit a church choir she had sung in for fifty years because she believed the whole congregation should join in singing together.

*Carol:* I remember my mother singing hymns as she cleaned; I remember Bible School projects and theological rigor in confirmation class, memorizing *verbatim* Luther's explanations of the commandments and the articles of the creed. I recall a story in *The Lutheran Standard* about four Gilbertson siblings attending Augustana College in Sioux Falls at the same time: me a freshman, Phil a sophomore, Mark a junior, and Dan a senior. I remember the spring of 1963, my freshman year, studying "The History of Christian Thought" with Professor Verlyn Smith and reading the early church theologians Augustine, Anselm, and Aquinas, as the history of *our* church. I was intrigued when Prof. Smith explained his invitation to serve as official observer to the Second Vatican Council; I remember his exhilarating account to the class when he returned from Rome, and my thrill to be touched by such a historic church moment. Teachers who led me through contemporary theologians from different traditions deepened my ecumenical understanding of faith's modern meanings.

And I remember that when I met Mark, I was struck that his family piety and ecumenical college experience oddly resonated with mine, though his family and college were Swiss, German, and German-Russian Catholic and mine were Norwegian Lutheran.

*Mark:* And, exploring together our pasts and our future, we made some discoveries. When I first visited Sioux Falls, I found not only a loving Christian home, but a familiar meal prayer, "Bless us, O Lord, and these thy gifts...." Carol only then discovered that her father, the South Dakota Lutheran Bishop, had introduced this prayer into their home years before, a by-product of his growing friendship with the local Catholic bishop, Bishop Hoch. Recalling my dad's relief when my two older brothers-in-law became Catholic when they married my sisters, I admired my father's ability to discover the humor in introducing my fiancé to his staunchly Catholic friends as a "bishop's daughter." I had known that my hometown Benedictine Abbey had become a center for Lutheran pastoral education and that my brothers there and their fellow monks had begun to meet area Lutheran pastors and that one of my most important high school teachers, someone who actually used the oral method to teach Latin! was actually teaching in the institute. But I didn't learn until then that the Western North Dakota's Lutheran bishop who supported these connections was Carol's uncle Roy.

*Carol:* I remember the first, breath-taking glimpse of the brick spires of Assumption Abbey soaring heavenward over the fields of wheat in Mark's hometown of Richardton, only a few prairie miles and a river's width from my birthplace in Crosby, North Dakota. The small, clapboard Lutheran church across the tracks made a humble statement, and it was dwarfed by the Abbey's magnificent declaration of God's presence on what I *had* thought of as the Lutheran plains. Years later I learned that the pastor of that small Lutheran church was the father of our Decorah friend Ruth Reitan. Recalling my father's pain that he could not officiate at my older brother's wedding to a Catholic in 1968, I was surprised at his delight to co-officiate with Mark's priest brother at our wedding seven years later. I recall my father's funeral in 1989, when nearly three hundred robed South Dakota clergy from all denominations triumphantly processed into the service, but I remember being particularly moved when a frail Bishop Hoch, in mitre and full regalia, entered the church and pushed his walker down the aisle to join the other clergy in the front.

So Mark and I tentatively began our ecumenical married life, gradually instructing ourselves in each other's traditions, trying to teach our children openness to different ways of encountering God's love, reminding them of their grandparents' fervent faith traditions. And God's unifying grace helped us, living in our family's prayers and our children's dual lives as Catholic schoolchildren and Lutheran choir members, as white-robed first communicants and participants in Lutheran mission trips, in their experience of their father as St. Benedict school board president and their mother as Board chair at the Lutheran School of Theology at Chicago.

In Martin Luther's discussion of the relationship of faith to good works, he likens the soul to iron: when exposed to fire, the cool, gray metal is metamorphosed into red-hot light. God's grace transforms the essence of the sinful, gray soul, and it is changed forever. But that transformation is not static: the red-hot soul, saved by grace, by its nature emanates heat and light it cannot avoid it. In the same way,

God's love moves out, through the believer's faithful soul, into the physical world in good works: prayer, meditation, confession, worship, and love and care for others.

In the same way, we hope our ecumenical union in marriage emanates out into our family's shared life and, we hope, into the way our children understand God's church and the Christian life. To use the words of the Strasbourg commentary on the Joint Declaration, we have tried to live in the understanding that "consensus can be elaborated in different ways;"[119] we have sought to live in the hope, as today's gospel reads, that we "may all be one." (John 17:21)

*Mark:* The Jesuit theologian Karl Rahner argues in *The Unity of the Church* that an ecumenical family symbolizes, on a local level, the wider church's unity, at the same time as it pushes a lagging church body towards that unity.

We cannot make those high claims for our marriage; we have been too busy struggling to balance our traditions and our lives to be either a symbol or a catalyst. God has helped us situate our daughters within the church's common theology while keeping alive two of its different, rich expressions. It wasn't always easy for our grade school children to arrive at afternoon choir practice at First Lutheran still wearing their blue uniforms from St. Benedict School. We have allowed ourselves to forget the jabs from their doctrinaire friends. Carol remembers our grade-school daughter leaning over during a service at First Lutheran to declare that her teacher had said that the Catholic Church was the one true church. We remember a daughter's embarrassment when she was asked how many sacraments there were, and she said "seven" rather than "two," or was it "two" rather than "seven"? But we also recall her fascination when she asked us exactly what a sacrament is, and I said, "A sacrament is an outward sign, instituted by Christ to give grace,"

*Carol:* ...and I said, "A sacrament is a visible means of grace, instituted by Christ."

For Luther and other church thinkers, human marriage is a visual image of the soul's union with Christ, just as for Rahner, ecumenical marriages symbolize hope for the church's future communion. But marriage unites two people who yet remain unique individuals; marriage does not dissolve differences any more than the Body of Christ consists only of hands.

*Mark:* For our children and for us, ecumenical family life has not been a blurring of traditions, but a dialogue between, a God-given chance to celebrate congruence and to clarify divergence. A God-given opportunity during their Confirmation for our daughters to learn, to their delight, that both Sunday services had the same liturgical structure, but a way, too, to learn the varied music of faith, to hear *both* concise homilies and impassioned sermons, to appreciate the mysterious spirituality of the Catholic Eucharistic mystery and the immediacy of spontaneous, contextualized Lutheran prayers, which sometimes included weather reports and travel schedules. We hope that our children are more theologically acute for needing to explain such differences to curious friends.

We don't know what the future holds for any of us, but we do know that God has poured out these gifts through the loving support of our pastors and fellow members at both our local parishes, and through the ecumenical emphasis at this college where we teach and the international church dialogues of this historic era. In a different time and place, our strong family histories might have forced us apart. Ours is not the whole story, and it is only one of many. But it is *one* concrete story of hope.

*Carol:* Each year, we go again as a family to immerse ourselves in the rich darkness, water, and fire of the St. Benedict Holy Saturday Evening service; and then when light dawns, we soar with the First Lutheran Easter trumpets and drums and the resounding declarations, "Christ is Risen!"

*Mark:* "He is Risen indeed!"

*Carol:* So we pray now, in the words of today's Gospel, "not only on behalf of those [here present], but also on behalf of those who will believe in [Christ] through [God's] word, that [we] may all be one." (John 17:20-21) We conclude with the prayer that ends the Joint Declaration itself; may it "rise before God like incense, the lifting up of our hands as the evening sacrifice."

*Mark:* "We give thanks to the Lord for this decisive step forward on the way to overcoming the division of the church. We ask the Holy Spirit to lead us further towards that visible unity which is Christ's will."

Chapter Four

# The Annual Ecumenical Lecture

## Introduction

**Ruth R. Kath**
*Luther College, Professor of German*

The presence of our speaker here at Luther College tonight is a dream finally come true, for me and for several other people on campus. One hot summer about six years ago, Study Abroad Director Mark Lund led Fr. Gary Krapfl and me on a very short, yet very long, whirlwind tour of Western Europe, in preparation for a new January Term course that Fr. Gary and I were beginning. The course was to explore the ecumenical relationship between Roman Catholics and Lutherans. As you might guess, we went first to Rome, Italy, and then to Wittenberg, Germany, home of the famous 95 Theses nailed to the door. But we also made a stop in Strasbourg, France. What has Strasbourg to do with the Roman Catholic-Lutheran dialogue? you might well ask. The answer was and is this: Everything. It was there, at the Ecumenical Research Institute associated with the Lutheran World Federation that the recently signed document between Catholics and Lutherans, the *Joint Declaration on the Doctrine of Justification*, was helped into existence, and there the work goes on. One of the people most crucial to its life is with us tonight.

At a little dinner that year, we met the very lively American director of the Institute. And we met a quiet German research professor from the University of Tübingen Seminary too. By the time we returned to Strasbourg with the Luther students that following January, the lively American had completed his term and returned to the United States, and the quiet German professor had become the new director. In 2000 and then again just a year ago, in 2002, the course became a pioneering effort, as the Luther students and I were joined by a faculty member and students from our Roman Catholic sister institution, Loras College in Dubuque, Iowa. The ecumenical group from both colleges, traveling, reflecting, and worshipping together, has been an enormous learning experience for us all. It has also been a groundbreaking one that has attracted the attention of the National Council of Catholic Bishops, the ELCA Office of Ecumenical Affairs in Chicago and the Lutheran World Federation in Geneva, Switzerland.

My good friend and Loras College colleague for the course, Fr. Douglas Wathier, has come all the way from Dubuque to be with us here tonight. He is accompanied by one of his students, junior Religious Studies major Nicole Reich, who was with us in Europe in 2002. I would ask them to stand, so that we might acknowledge their contribution and thank them for their presence with us tonight.

So, this is the way the course goes: first a week in Rome, then a week in Wittenberg, and then Strasbourg. Strasbourg is always at the end of the three-week study tour. At that last stop, students see the beautiful city and its medieval Cathedral, but it is most especially the Ecumenical Institute and its director Theo Dieter that regularly prove to be among the greatest highlights of the trip. Students tell us this: They have studied about ecumenism in Rome, and begun to experience ecumenism in Wittenberg, but it is in Theo Dieter in Strasbourg that the whole ecumenical experience gets a human face: a person who not only talks about ecumenism, harmony among the Christians of the world, but who has dedicated his life to it, out of intellectual conviction and deep faith. The encounter changes them, and I think you will find out in a minute just why.

The lecture this evening is sponsored by the Lecture and Fine Arts Committee and 1979 Luther alumnus Mark Gould and his wife Karen. Dr. Dieter's lecture tonight begins his three-week residency as a Program Visitor here under the auspices of the Sense of Vocation program. Theo will be a guest in many classes on the campus, as well as meet with students interested in church leadership and ministry, a weekly ecumenical discussion group, alumni, two groups of area pastors, local retired clergy, the Rotary Club, the Pericope group, and will also preach in several area churches and in the Luther Chapel in early March. In his spare time he is available for conversation with students and faculty. He has been here in Decorah a scant twenty-four hours, but it is good to see that he has already embraced the work ethic for which Luther College is famous!

For six years, I have dreamed of bringing this extraordinary man to Iowa to share him with all of you. Tonight, that dream has finally come true. Theo, I am more delighted to have you here than I can possibly express. Please join me in welcoming Dr. Theodor Dieter, who will speak to us about "The Vocation of an Ecumenist."

## Vocation as Ecumenist—Ecumenism as Vocation

**Theodor Dieter** ,
*Director of the Institute for Ecumenical Research, Strasbourg, France*

In Strasbourg (France), where I come from, there is a magnificent cathedral. When visitors come to our Institute for Ecumenical Research, e.g., students from Luther College, together with Prof. Ruth Kath, I sometimes offer a guided tour of this wonderful building. Standing in front of this church I draw attention to the fact that nearly no one of the hundreds of workers who built the cathedral could see this building finished. It took more than three hundred years before it came to completion. People tell the story that once three craftsmen working at the cathedral were asked what they did. The first craftsman answered, "I cut stones." The second one responded, "I earn money." But the third one said, "I participate in building the cathedral." He had a vision, and he participated in the vision the architects had. Even if this third craftsman did nothing more than cut one stone after the other, everything he did was meaningful. He regarded all that he did as a contribution to building a wonderful house where God the creator was celebrated by demonstrating all human skills, where people could encounter Christ in his mercy and strength, and where the Holy Spirit was experienced in manifold ways. Again, our craftsman perhaps did nothing more than cut stones, but because he sensed his vocation to contribute to

Theodor Dieter

realizing the fascinating vision of the cathedral, everything that he did was meaningful.

The third craftsman of this very short story is a good model for an Ecumenist. Who of us will see the unity of the Church become visible? Who of us will sit at the Lord's table celebrating Holy Supper with equal participation of Lutherans, Catholics, Methodists, and Orthodox? Does it make sense to commit yourself to a work in which progress depends so heavily on developments and decisions of so many church bodies over which you have little or even no influence? It may happen that Ecumenists work for years to enable the churches to take one step towards visible unity; they pray and study together, they seek to clarify problems in numerous conversations, and eventually a synod decides after an emotional discussion to go instead in another direction. Is it responsible to spend a considerable amount of one's lifetime in a project whose outcome is so unpredictable and uncertain? Thus it is a serious question whether one truly has a call to serve as an Ecumenist. Experiencing such a call can give one a clear orientation, motivation, and strength in going forward, as well as in suffering setbacks. The time of a good-weather-Ecumenism is over. Committing yourself and your lifetime for the Ecumenical Movement requires a strong sense of vocation!

My presentation will contain three parts. First, I would like to reflect on what "vocation" means. Second, I will talk about my vocation as Ecumenist, and, third, I will raise the question of the churches' vocation to ecumenism and give an example for it.

I. What is "vocation"? Let us take a few minutes to reflect on the history of the concept itself. We will see that an ecumenical problem is hidden behind this concept. According to the New Testament, all Christians have received a calling. 1 Cor 1:9: "God is faithful; by him you were called into the fellowship of his Son, Jesus Christ our Lord." Paul continues, "to those who are the called, both Jews and Greeks, Christ [is] the power of God, and the wisdom of God." (1 Cor 1:24) This spiritual calling is directed to freedom: "For you were called to freedom, brothers and sisters," Paul states (Gal 5:13), and there is a danger that Christians desert "the one who called you in the grace of Christ." (Gal 1:6) In the time of the New Testament, Christians experienced this calling deeply since it meant conversion from paganism or from the Jewish religion to Christian faith. This was a personal, individual vocation which took place in a definite way in baptism. But in the course of time, this experience of a personal vocation began to fade away. Thus in the Middle Ages "vocation" was related to the calling to a monastic life. Again, this was a personal experience changing life deeply. In late Medieval times, a few mystics began to talk about a calling even for daily office and work, but it was clear for them that the calling to which monks and nuns responded had a much higher status than the calling to normal work.

Martin Luther changed this understanding deeply. Since, as he taught, we are saved and justified by God's grace alone and by faith alone, a difference in our status in life makes no difference before God. Luther talked of a spiritual vocation which every Christian receives through baptism and to which he or she responds by faith, one that makes him or her a priest in the sense of the common priesthood of all baptized. Together with this vocation every Christian receives a calling to serve the neighbor at the place where one lives and works. All Christians are called to practice their daily tasks, as well as their professional work as service to others. In doing so, they are co-workers with God. In this respect there is no difference between the works of a farm girl or a servant and the works of a prince. Over against God, it is only important whether these works are done with love, faithfulness, and diligence, or not, simply responding to God's love and not trying to earn this love by good works. In this way profession and vocation come together. In the German language of Luther's time, especially because of his Bible translation and some of his writings, the word "Beruf" came to contain both vocation and profession, and the term comes from "vocation." Thus the term "vocation" was no longer restricted to monastic life but was related to the daily work of all Christians. Subsequently the idea spread in the world that a profession is not only a means to earn money, but also the place and the way to realize a calling by God.

For Luther, professional activity understood as vocation does not aim at crossing social borders or making a career, even if he does not exclude that something like this can happen. One receives God's vocation in whatever station in life one finds oneself, according to Paul's words, (1 Cor 7:20-24): "Let each of you remain in the condition in which you were called" [this calling means the vocation to be a Christian]. Were you a slave when called? Do not be concerned about it. Even if you can gain your freedom, make use of your present condition now more than ever...In whatever condition you were called, brothers and sisters, there remain with God." This is very difficult for us to hear! We see how deeply our present society is different from the societies at the time of Paul or Luther. We live in a world of rapid change, and hardly anyone chooses the profession of his or her father or mother simply because it is their father's or mother's. But this creates a profound difficulty for us when we struggle with the concept of vocation: To what are we called by God? Luther could say: Regard the social place where you live as the place where God wants you to serve your neighbor. But we have to ask: Which is the place where we can serve others, because there are thousands of possible places, and no one is determined for us by social circumstances.

This really creates a problem for the idea of vocation. Vocation means that it is not our decision where we see the main tasks of our lives, what we regard as the purpose of our lives. We look for our destiny, and we may find it or miss it. But we do not decide about our vocation. Otherwise we could not say: He missed his vocation. If it is a matter of decision, it is impossible to miss a vocation. But if a vocation is to be found or received you can miss it, either by not hearing the calling, or by not responding positively to it. Nowadays, however, we ourselves decide where we work and what kind of work we will do, what kind of lives we should lead. Where is the place of a vocation in such a context?

I would like to mention another change in the concept of vocation. In the eighteenth century people tended to forget that God is the one who calls. Thus when they heard the word "vocation" or "inner vocation" they just thought of having the disposition for something by nature. One should choose a profession in which he or she can realize his or her inclination and gifts of nature. Otherwise we would say: They have missed their vocation. Here we can see that spiritual vocation has been reduced to inclination and talent. A person was considered extremely fortunate if his or her profession completely corresponded to the inner vocation (his or her inclination and talent).

As a result of our reflection on the concept of vocation we should first note that our profession can be the place of our vocation by God if others benefit from what we do and if we do not harm others. Second, in a world of rapid social change we cannot, as Luther did, regard the place where we live and work directly as the place of our vocation. As a reaction to this, the term "vocation," as understood by many people, is no longer related to God's calling, but to our inner inclinations and talents which we wish to realize in our profession. Third, if we as

Christians want to continue to use the concept of vocation in relation to our profession, we will have to consider carefully our own personal history and try to discern whether there are trajectories that point in a certain direction, experience ourselves in communication with others and find out where we have the clear feeling that something that we do is simply O.K. and meaningful. But above all, we should try to get acquainted with the voice of God by attentively listening to his word.

**II.** Now, I come to my second part. I was asked to say something about my way to Ecumenism. I would like to mention this, because without this invitation I would not use the occasion of this meeting to talk about myself. But perhaps this is an example how to find one's vocation.

I studied Protestant Theology and Philosophy. In philosophy, it was Aristotle, the Greek philosopher, whose works I studied for years, while in theology my main interest was directed to Martin Luther and his theology. By this simple fact, my ecumenical engagement was so to speak predestined. Of course, I knew nothing about this. I simply had excellent teachers who offered lectures and seminars in Aristotle, and others who gave challenging lectures on Martin Luther. The reason why this constellation finally led into Ecumenism is that Martin Luther was a very sharp critic of Aristotle. But I found many insights in Aristotle that were convincing to me, and I did not want to lose them while doing theology. I could not give them up without compromising my intellectual integrity. For me, Aristotle represented in an excellent way what human beings could know without the aid of revelation. I could not believe that Theology could benefit by ignoring such an outstanding philosopher. But Luther attacked Aristotle for having tempted Christian theologians to abandon a biblically based theology. Instead, as he complained, these theologians studied Aristotle and spent years of precious time discussing problems raised by a dead pagan who did not even know that the world was created by God and had a beginning and an end and that the human soul is immortal. In doing so, these theologians became arrogant and excessively self-confident. They claimed to be able to understand, explain and argue for even what happens in the Eucharist, they developed a theory of changing the elements, using Aristotle's terms like "substance" and "accident," in the so-called theory of transubstantiation.

However, I was deeply impressed by Martin Luther. When I studied his commentary on Paul's letter to the Romans I could follow the way this young theologian step by step developed his theology. I could hardly believe that a young man could bring together so many different insights and marveled at the way he wove together the different strands of his thoughts with the traditions he had learned, developing at the same time a very new way of doing theology. I admired his creativity, finding new and unexpected ways to see things and to gain new insights from the Bible and elaborating convincing critical arguments against many theological traditions.

I carefully followed the lines of his thought and his developments, asking so often: When did Luther find his decisive breakthrough by which he became the Reformer? What is the precise content of this breakthrough? When did he become non-Catholic? My teacher had the idea that only this is Lutheran, which is non-Catholic, and thus leads to a break with the Catholics or is the result of this break. Lutheran identity was defined for me by being non-Catholic. The liberals among my colleagues sometimes smiled and said: Isn't it rather old-fashioned to spend so much time inquiring after Lutheran identity? But I was convinced that Luther's findings in reading the Bible were so revealing that it is important for any theology to deal with them. I have still this conviction. But there happened a decisive change in viewing Lutheran identity.

When I was preparing for my examination, I studied a one thousand page book on the Doctrine of Justification in Martin Luther and Thomas Aquinas written by a Dominican, Otto Hermann Pesch. He was and still is fascinated by Thomas Aquinas as well as by Martin Luther. He explained how different Thomas and Luther are in their way of thinking, their theological style and approach to theology, how different in utilizing concepts with the result that these concepts have different meanings to them. Taking this into account, Pesch showed that there is much common ground between these theologians, so that from the position of the one there can be no simple condemnation of the other. It took me three months to read this book carefully. The more I read this book, the more I became convinced that Pesch's interpretations of both theologians was right, and that his approach is very forward-looking. After having read this book I had to stop thinking that Lutheran identity could only be defined in opposition to Catholicism. On the contrary, if there is indeed so much common ground, then Lutheran identity must be misinterpreted when it is construed so strongly in opposition to Catholicism. This is true, even given the fact that Luther and some elements of his theology were excluded from the Catholic Church, which by so doing became the Roman-Catholic Church. If Lutheranism is defined by its opposition to the Catholic Church, then it must hope and wish that this church does not change, because then the identity of Lutheranism would also change, since both are bound together by opposition. To the contrary, it should be the honor of Lutheran Theology to find a positive self-definition by being in accordance with Scripture. Then Lutheran Theology can welcome every other church which also shows its faithfulness to Scripture.

After this great experience, intellectual as well as spiritual, I started my studies on Luther and Aristotle. I studied Luther's quotations from Aristotle and his comments on his teachings. Often, I found that Luther misunderstood Aristotle. But I could not imagine that a theologian who was such a genius could make so many mistakes in interpreting Aristotelian texts. Thus I asked: How did he know about Aristotle? I studied many of the thousands of commentaries written in medieval universities in order to understand Aristotle. Which Aristotle is it whom Luther knew and criticized? I found: It is not Aristotle as we read him nowadays; it is Aristotle as interpreted and commented on by medieval authors. Thus my research on Luther's criticism of Aristotle led me deep into the world of medieval thinking. The conflict between Luther and Aristotle motivated me to study medieval theologies and philosophies which were to become so important for the Catholic tradition.

Again, I had the experience that many of the texts of medieval authors, mainly those of Thomas Aquinas, became increasingly convincing to me. And Thomas used the philosophy of Aristotle to explain what Christians believe! Did Luther really criticize what I thought was correct? What would this mean?

Thus I had a closer look to see what the target of Luther's criticism really was. I got deeper into the manifold theologies of the Middle Ages and found that Luther's critical remarks do not meet all these theologies in the same way, but that only some of those theologians actually taught what Luther so strongly rejected. Then I tried to find out which arguments Luther used in his polemics against the Scholastics, the School or university theologians of his time and their predecessors. Many Protestant researchers only describe Luther's thoughts implicitly assuming that what he says is the truth. To say this seems to be very unfair, but I myself was astonished when I saw that this is actually the case. If you read books on Luther and ask if the authors check the validity of his arguments you will find in most cases that they do not. I could not be content by simply stating: But Luther said! In a medieval disputation, and Luther liked these disputations very much, one had to present arguments. Thus I went deeper into Luther's theology looking for reasons for his criticism against some medieval theologies. And I could find them, so that I tried to establish so to speak a medieval disputation by discussing arguments of both sides forth and back. Proceeding this way I gained some insights in Luther's theology which I would never have found if I had worked in a more traditional way. If I call it an ecumenical approach to take seriously the truth claims of both sides which are in conflict, then this ecumenical methodology helped me better to understand not only the other side, but also Luther's theology. A really ecumenical approach helps you to understand your own tradition better.

What I have described is an essential part of my own discovery of my inner vocation to be an Ecumenist. As soon as you realize that there are true understandings and insights also in other churches, but these insights are expressed, spelled out and reflected upon in ways different from your own, you must become something like an Ecumenist, because all truth is one, even if there are different perspectives from which to approach the truth. All Christian theologians claim to talk about the Triune God, the Father, who sent his Son for the salvation of the world, and the Holy Spirit who makes Christ present among us. Therefore we cannot be satisfied with a, so to speak, Frank-Sinatra-Doctrine of truth: I do it my way, you do it your way, saying: This is my truth, and that is your truth, even if there are tensions or contradictions between them. Truth reveals what is the case with the triune God, and this is common to all of us Christians. On the other hand we look at the truth in different perspectives, and we cannot reduce the multitude of these perspectives to one. There is one truth but manifold perspectives; this constitutes the ecumenical problem in a nutshell. What I have described reflects my own experience over many years.

**III.** The third part of my presentation is the vocation of the churches for Ecumenism. As history and present observations show, we cannot take the ecumenical commitment of the churches for granted. If the churches have to act under pressure in their societies they tend to reflect on their core competence, i.e., that which makes them different from other churches. By emphasizing this they hope to gain strength. They behave like business companies even if they are not really "in business." Looking for a niche in the religious "market," they de-emphasize what they have in common with other Christian churches. Thus it is necessary also to talk about the vocation of the Christian churches for Ecumenism.

The basic problem of Ecumenism is not that the unity of the Church is so far away and could be established only by powerful actions on our side. On the contrary, *the unity of the Church is already given*. It is given by the one Lord to whom we are connected by baptism and by faith. There is already one body, just as there is one Lord. The unity of the body of Christ is nothing we Christians have to accomplish; it is given to us as a gift of our risen Lord. This is the *Ecumenical indicative*. But we Christians live in communities, which separate themselves from one another. Thus the unity of the body of Christ is given, but it does not become visible and is not lived out in the world. Thus there is an internal self-contradiction in all Christian churches. All of them belong to the body of Christ, but in spite of this fact they do not pray together or celebrate Eucharist together. Thus the *Ecumenical imperative* is: Live what you already are: the one body of Christ!

Let us have a look at the Roman Catholic Church. In Vatican Council II it was stated that by baptism in the Triune God we are united with Christ and are integrated in his body, so that even non-Roman Catholics deserve the honorary name of a Christian. This is the case even if some Christians belong only to the so-called ecclesial communities. That means that the body of Christ is much more comprehensive than the Roman Catholic Church. We should keep this in mind, since it is a consequence of what is explicitly stated in the Council. When it now comes to celebrating Eucharist together with Catholic and Non-Catholic Christians then the Catholic documents argue: Eucharist as a sacrament does not only effect unity among Christians but it signifies the unity of the Church. When Christians who belong to different churches are gathered around the Lord's table then they suffer a contradiction. Sharing the Eucharist would signify, "We are one body." But since these Christians belong to churches which do not live in church fellowship they are in fact not one body. In order to avoid this contradiction it is better not to celebrate Eucharist together. This is the official argument.

However, this is only one half of the truth, and Catholic representatives often forget the other part. What does the Eucharist symbolize? It is a sign of the unity of the body of Christ. Now we have seen that according to Vatican Council II the body of Christ is more comprehensive than the Roman-Catholic Church. But in principle all the non-Catholic members of the body of Christ are excluded from participating in the Roman-Catholic Eucharist even if they belong to the body of Christ. At least, this is the case with the Christians of the Reformation churches. The consequence of this is that no Catholic Eucharist is able to be a sign of the unity of the body of Christ. This may be a shocking judgment for Catholics but it is an inevitable consequence of the fact that on the one hand, Catholics admit that non-Catholics are also members of the body of Christ, on the other hand they exclude in principle all Christians from the Eucharist whose churches are not in union with them. Thus it follows that every Roman-Catholic Eucharist suffers a defect, as do the Eucharistic celebrations of other churches who exclude other Christians.

I would very much like to stress that the split between the churches affects their substance, since Eucharist is at the center of the Church. This is true even if the Catholic position says that the body of Christ, the church we confess as the one, holy, catholic and apostolic church, is realized in the Roman-Catholic Church (the famous *subsistit* of *Lumen Gentium*). But the Ecumenical problem results exactly from the fact that, as the Council itself admits, the body of Christ is more comprehensive than the Roman-Catholic Church. There are only two possibilities. Either the Roman Catholic Church is strictly identical with the body of Christ. Then there exists no Ecumenical problem; Ecumenism would not be a possibility for the Roman Catholic Church. Or it is not simply identical, and then we have an Ecumenical problem, which touches also the substance of the Catholic Eucharist.

We have seen: The Ecumenical vocation of the Christian churches results from the contradiction that, on the one hand, we Christians have *one* Lord, and that *the unity of his body is given to us*, but that, on the other hand, *the churches do not live this given unity of the one church* and Christians cannot experience it.

One main area which hinders churches from living the given unity is doctrine. Doctrine sometimes appears as old-fashioned, merely a remote intellectual problem. But doctrine is pretty much important, since as we think about God so he appears to us. Please compare this with a situation familiar to us: If we, for example, have wrong thoughts about a person, we can hardly deal properly with him or her. The same is true in relation to God. Therefore the churches have had good reasons to take doctrinal questions seriously. Doctrinal shortcomings may endanger the good relationship to God, and thus they can become a question of life and death. This is especially true with the doctrine of justification. At the time of the Reformation, the conflict about this doctrine led to the split of Western Christianity. In our time, major ecumenical progress was made in overcoming these controversies by signing the so-called "Joint Declaration on the Doctrine of Justification" (JDDJ) in Augsburg (Germany) in 1999. To conclude my talk, I would like to give you a short report about this project since our Institute was involved in it. Here we find a good example that churches took their vocation of Ecumenism seriously.

For centuries the doctrine of justification was a matter of sharp controversies, was even the background for wars in Europe. During the last fifty years, Catholic and Protestant theologians increasingly tried to understand the position of the other church more correctly, carefully avoiding misinterpretations, and looking for common ground. In Europe, the situation had deeply changed by World War II. In the distress and difficulties of the war as well as in the opposition against Hitler, many Catholics and Protestants discovered that they both were Christians believing in the same God. After the war, a few million refugees came to the West. Thus many areas where for centuries only Protestants or only Catholics had lived became mixed areas with regard to confession. People belonging to different churches got acquainted with one another, and more and more people entered into mixed marriages. Many theological studies were undertaken in order to clarify the controversial problems, in the United States as well as in Europe. The Second Vatican Council established a new openness and an enormous interest in Ecumenism on the Catholic side. Many theologians gained the conviction that in the doctrine of justification there can be found so much common ground that there is no valid reason to continue condemning the other church's doctrine as heretical or Church dividing. But strictly speaking, these were private opinions of theologians even when they were well founded. Skeptics often raised the question: But what do the churches think about this? What is their official stance on this? On behalf of the Lutheran World

Federation and the Catholic Church, a few Lutheran and Catholic theologians made the attempt to summarize the result of various dialogues and produce a paper on which the churches could officially act. But how to do this? On the one side there was the Roman Catholic Church with one Magisterium in Rome. On the other hand there were some 120 Lutheran churches gathered in the LWF but each of them with its own authority to make doctrinal decisions. Would a process leading to a signing of the common document be possible if the partners were so extremely different? With the first mailing of the JDDJ the churches were asked to react. The LWF received some dozen responses proposing changes and criticizing some wordings or even whole paragraphs. Our Institute was asked to analyze these responses and bring them together in a small study so that representatives of the LWF could again negotiate the text trying to present all the concerns of Lutheran churches to the Catholics. By means of our paper the responding Lutheran churches sat at the table, too. Also the Catholics had a long list of proposed changes or criticisms. Thus there was much to do in two meetings in Wuerzburg (Germany). My American colleague, Michael Root, and I participated on behalf of our Institute. The astonishing thing was: It worked. It was possible to bring the concerns of all the responding churches on the table. The great number of Lutheran churches was not an obstacle in the way of fruitful negotiations. When the final text was mailed, the Lutheran churches and the Magisterium of the Catholic church were asked finally to make up their mind and say "Yes" or "No" to the document. A "Yes" meant (1) that they stated that in the document a consensus on basic truths of the doctrine of justification has been reached (in spite of some remaining differences), and (2) that therefore the condemnations of the Reformation Era do not apply to the Catholic or Lutheran doctrine as explained in the document. Again, our Institute was asked by the LWF to evaluate the responses of the churches as the basis for the decision of the Council of the LWF.

This was very difficult since many churches did not simply say "Yes" or "No" but wrote long texts, commenting on numerous aspects. In a few cases we wondered and discussed for a long time whether a response should be counted as "Yes" or "No" or as both, "Yes" *and* "No." Eventually, the Council of the LWF unanimously accepted the JDDJ on behalf of the LWF and the consenting Lutheran churches. This is a very significant result in view of the great number and variety of the

Lutheran churches worldwide. It could only be reached by innumerable discussions and fierce debates.

All the more, it was a shock that the Roman-Catholic response released only two weeks later was so ambiguous, saying "Yes" and "No" at the same time. Obviously, there was a split within the Catholic Magisterium, the Congregation for the Doctrine of the Faith in Rome. In this case, even having one Magisterium did not allow the Roman-Catholic Church to respond as unanimously as the one hundred twenty Lutheran churches had done. I am convinced that it was Pope John Paul II himself who decided that this response could not be the last word from the Catholic side. So again, we entered into negotiations with the Catholic Church which led to the so-called Annex. By adding this Annex, the JDDJor, more precisely, the Official Common Statement confirming the JDDJ "in its entirety" could be signed. This event of Augsburg 1999 is an Ecumenical quantum leap. For the first time, the Catholic Church and non-Catholic churches made an *official* doctrinal statement by which they *mutually acknowledge* their respective doctrines even if they do not totally agree. Now that this remarkable step has been taken, it is not clear what the next steps should be. On the contrary, we have to struggle to avoid setbacks. Thus I come back to the third craftsman I mentioned at the beginning. A clear sense of vocation is needed to remain committed to the Ecumenical work. Then we will be able to enjoy progress as well as suffer setbacks, always convinced that we participate in the work of building the Ecumenical cathedral in which we Christians will live and experience together the unity of the Church which God has already given to us in Jesus Christ.

Chapter Five

# Ecumenism at Home and Abroad

## Ecumenical Partnership in Ministry

**Rev. Dr. Gary F. Krapfl**
St. Benedict Church & Luther College

I recently took a sabbatical leave after more than thirty years of campus and parish ministry. One of the components of the leave was the opportunity for me to visit a number of college campuses in the Midwest where partnership in ministry exists between ELCA Lutherans and Catholics. One of these visits took place on a very pleasant and sunny fall day, the last one of October, the actual Reformation Day in history, being observed as Founder's Day on this campus at the regularly scheduled morning chapel service. The 10:00AM gathering included hymns, prayers, a sermon, and the presentation of awards to distinguished employees of this college in recognition and appreciation for their years of loyal service.

The President was the chosen speaker for the chapel service. In his prepared text, he said that one of the advantages of working at a church-related college was that a person of faith could combine vocation with work. Out of this combination would arise passion—the ability to combine faith and service in life in a way that inspires accomplishment and motivates an energy to devote oneself wholeheartedly to one's work.

The insight was clear and immediate; the word "passion" perfectly describes my interest in and desire to continue ecumenical partnership in ministry. Passion underlies what is going on today, but the interest and desire have been part of me for most of my life, and only fully experienced in the years I have been in Decorah with ministry at both St. Benedict Church and Luther College.

Growing up in an area with a high percentage of Catholics in eastern Iowa, I can remember a fascination I had while riding in the family car by one of the "other" churches while on the way to Mass at our own. Though the actual words were never spoken, the attitude that was conveyed by my parents and the parish was that while it was nice that those other people were gathering for worship in their church, it wasn't the same as what we were doing because we were the real church and they were not. I wondered what they were doing and what was so different about their time in church that supposedly made what we were doing so much the better and when could I find out some more about these people who were religiously different from us?

I had to wait until seminary to first have that experience. At the time (the late 1960's) Aquinas Institute in Dubuque had begun a cooperative effort with the Lutheran and Presbyterian seminaries located in the same city. Some of our core courses were open to students of all three Schools. From these courses, I became aware of the "shared history" among Christian Churches, and the insights that developed from this truth began their intellectual formulation within me.

Time spent in graduate school in Washington, DC, with a summer of classes at Wesley Seminary and seminars with a wide variety of ordained men and women who were both faculty and students was another significant experience. Experiences in Cedar Rapids as a chaplain on two campuses with a larger number of people from traditions other than Catholic, as well as membership in a Jewish-Christian dialogue were the last in a series of ministerial preparations for coming to Decorah in 1990 with an eagerness for and a readiness to respond to the passion for life and work in this unique setting.

That there was a wonderful ecumenical spirit among the churches and people of Decorah was no secret. I was aware of the pioneer movement in ecumenism that had begun soon after the close of Vatican Council II with the faculty exchange program between the

Benedictine monks at St. John's Collegeville in Minnesota and the religion department at Luther College. When that was no longer possible for understandable reasons, none of which included problems or difficulties of ecumenical interest, the effort was continued by one whose name and influence still live on. I had heard of the presence of Emeric Lawrence, O.S.B., the warm reception he was extended by not only the college but also the parish and others who knew him, and the impact he had upon people who, when hearing what kinds of cooperation he was engaged in with Catholics and Lutherans, would question their own thinking and experience. When his terms here had been completed, the class that he taught and the ministry he provided was assumed by the priests and staff of St. Benedict's, and those possibilities made relocation to Decorah a very attractive offer for me.

Today, the partnership has developed to include a number of experiences. I am a regular on the schedule for morning chapel with the college pastors, taking the role of liturgist one day a week and that of preacher whenever asked. Each semester a combined ecumenical liturgy is celebrated—the annual "Walk to Church" Sunday on the first weekend of the Fall semester and the evening Ash Wednesday Service to begin the season of Lent where Lutheran and Catholic students, faculty, and staff combine for the roles of liturgical service while retaining distinct approaches to Eucharist within the same setting. In addition to being the designated chaplain for Catholic students, I am also the on-call pastor for the entire college community when needed. Following in the footsteps of Fr. Emeric, I teach the course on Catholic Life & Thought in the second semester of each academic year, as has been the custom for more than thirty-five years.

The Ecumenical Lecture Series started shortly after my arrival as a cooperative effort between Luther College and St. Benedict Parish. The annual event held each spring has brought a variety of speakers to campus from Lutheran and Catholic circles, as well as the Muslim and Jewish Traditions. A highlight was the joint appearance of Archbishop Oscar Lipscomb of Mobile, AL, and Bishop H. George Anderson of the ELCA to speak about the *Joint Declaration on Justification*—a project both of them had been part of during their terms on the Lutheran-Catholic Dialogue in the United States. This was followed by an ecumenical service of vespers celebrating the signing of that document with persons from both traditions present on that October night in 1999. A further development of this interest was the development of a January term study abroad course by Dr. Ruth Kath and me which studied the sacred spaces of Lutherans and Catholics in Rome, Wittenberg, Berlin, Cologne, and Strasbourg, and which attracted twenty-one students in its inaugural year.

Off-campus, parish ministry in this area, with churches from a variety of Christian traditions, provides many opportunities for ecumenical cooperation. While the majority of these have been with the pastors of other Lutheran churches, I have also been present for joint services with Methodist, United Church of Christ, and Covenant Church pastors in their churches as well as in St. Benedict's. Many of these events represent the variety of faith experiences celebrated in human life—baptisms, weddings, and funerals, to name those most often scheduled. At least once each year, I am also invited to be present for a wedding of a former Luther student or alum, representing the Catholic presence in an ecumenical marriage.

While the above represents a summary of the positive aspects of this partnership, there are several areas of concern that present challenges for the future. Conversations and cooperation with clergy and members of the ELCA churches in this area reveal a certain skepticism with regard to the seriousness of the Catholic Church to full and visible unity of churches within the Body of Christ. They have retained in their ecclesial memory the ways that Martin Luther and his early followers were treated by Rome and the Catholics of that era, and the subsequent attitude of their needing to "return" to the Church in the centuries which followed. The Princeton Proposal for Christian Unity and the study of the concept of *koinonia*, or fellowship, when all the churches will be able to recognize in one another the one, holy, catholic, and apostolic church in all its fullness, as a foundation for future partnership impact my passion about hope for the future.

In this parish, there are some who are very excited about the progress that has been made, especially with the Lutheran churches, and wonder if full and visible unity will happen in their lifetimes. There are others who still believe the Catholic Church alone to be the one true Church of Christ and want those who belong to other churches to recant and repent before being welcomed into one church. I have a sense that the same range of thinking is likely found among some Lutherans as well. A word used to describe this problem concerning progress made at some levels and unwillingness to move on other levels is "reception."

As a pastor, it is important for me to have the awareness that not all members of the congregation of St. Benedict Church are at the same level of ecumenical interest and cooperation as I am. As a leader, it is necessary for me to stress the importance of this aspect of church life and to reassure the hesitant that ecumenical progress has the approval of our church's highest authorities. As a teacher, I must involve as many as I can in the reception process and be aware of opportunities to point out that this learning process is by its very nature not exclusively concerned with theological documents alone, but also developments in the areas of liturgy, pastoral care, canon law, church practices and customs, and personal spirituality. To celebrate the progress is only part of the process; to increase the level of reception is also necessary, and probably the more difficult task.

During those sabbatical months mentioned at the beginning of this essay, I did have the opportunity to visit several other church-related colleges to have a first-hand look at what was happening at other schools of comparable size and similarity to Luther College. Most Catholic colleges do have a course in the catalogue on the Reformation and the churches which trace their origin from that event. Most Lutheran colleges do have a course on Catholicism or ecumenical progress. Some do have the part-time presence of a Catholic on the Lutheran campus, and others have some kind of arrangement with a local parish to provide for the needs of Catholic students. No other college has the kind of situation and cooperation that exists here, and I came home with a much greater appreciation for my place of work and enjoyment.

The passion that one has to do something does not always assure that the energy expended will have any kind of lasting effect on those involved. When such affirmation and confirmation is received, it makes all the effort worthwhile and expands the desire even more. I recently received an invitation to be present for another wedding which included these words:

> We're not sure if you remember us, but you certainly had a lasting impact on the two of us. Two years ago we took your Catholic Life and Thought class together on campus. At that point in our relationship we were both struggling with our beliefs and we knew that this would become an issue later in our lives. Matt had a Catholic upbringing and Kelly was considering the idea of converting to Catholicism. Kelly then met

with you outside of class a few times and we both began attending some of the St. Ben's services. We took that class together only about a year into our relationship and we would both agree that it was an experience that greatly strength ened and enriched our relationship.

Our faith is extremely important to both of us, and although we have come from different backgrounds, we know that our core values are the same. Over time we have decided that neither of us will be converting to a new faith. Through your teachings we have learned to embrace our upbringings while at the same time we have found ways to bring our values together as a guide for how we would like to live as a couple and someday raise our children.

The connection that we feel with you is something that we are so grateful for. Perhaps without your even realizing it, your teachings and influence have meant so much to us.

What else could one say but SOLI DEO GLORIA!

## Among the Sacred Spaces

*That they all may be one*: John 17:21

Ruth R. Kath
Luther College

The course "Sacred Spaces of Western Europe: Italy and Germany" is designed to address the extraordinary international agreement between Lutheran and Roman Catholics, the Joint Declaration on the Doctrine of Justification. Fr. Gary Krapfl and I began the course in 1999 solely as a Luther College offering. It developed in 2000 into a joint effort between faculty and students of Luther College and our Roman Catholic sister institution Loras College of Dubuque, Iowa. My friend and former professor, Fr. Douglas Wathier, S.T.D., Chair of Loras' Department of Religious Studies is co-leader. The popular biennial course draws students of many faith traditions together for an on-site introduction to ecumenical formation. The following represents the experiences of one recent January Term study tour.

It was an unusually ecumenical group that boarded the plane with us in Chicago that year: Among the students from both schools were five ELCA Lutherans, three Catholics, two Missouri Synod Lutherans (LCMS), one Methodist, and a Wisconsin Synod (WELS) member. Luther students and faculty were traveling during the regular three and a half week January Term, but the Loras contingent had no such luxury: they had given up their Christmas Break to make the trip and would return to their campus just hours before the beginning of their spring semester in mid-January.

It is custom to depart for Europe with the combined group just two days after Christmas. We embarked on the trip that year in anticipation of the legendary warmth of Rome, and of the renowned

New Year's Eve celebration in St. Peter's Square. By the time the leaders finished introductions, the students were eagerly looking forward to that special celebration in the company of thousands of other visitors from all over the world.

Our group traveled first to Rome and Assisi, Italy, then to Wittenberg, Germany, with a short side trip to Berlin, and concluded in Strasbourg, France. We made. In Rome over five days, we began the course by visiting sites, such as the Vatican and the famous Sistine Chapel, which are strongly identified with the Roman Catholic Church today. Along the way our students learned to identify the ornate Baroque style of architecture throughout Vatican City and Rome, preferred by Italian church architects of the sixteenth century because it demonstrated the glory of the Catholic Church, in direct reaction to the Reformation. Our students were overwhelmed by the size and elaborateness of St. Peter's Basilica.

While the group saw most of the usual Roman attractions, the special focus in Rome was on sites that represent the shared history of all Christians, those places that defined the church at its earliest beginnings, and through some twelve centuries until the Reformation in the sixteenth century. One of the most moving of these sites is located in eight miles of ancient tunnels below the bustling city. The Catacombs of St. Priscilla are where the earliest Roman Christians buried their dead, they also gathered there to remember them in worship on their feast days and anniversaries. Dimly lit, the walls of the catacombs contain remnants of precious frescoes that tell the ancient biblical stories common to all Christians. On this trip, our Italian guide showed us a special fresco of the Christ Child with his mother Mary. The pair is flanked by an ancient prophet pointing above to the bright star of Bethlehem—a foretelling of the coming of the Son of God. Approximately 1600 years old, this fresco is among the earliest known images of Mary and her child, yet judging from the faces of our students, it deeply touches modern Christians who descend the stairs into the dark catacombs of Rome today.

Closer to the center of Rome we went underground again, this time to view the little-known *Scavi*, the excavation site directly beneath St. Peter's Basilica in the Vatican. Only 100 people a day are allowed down into the *Scavi*, a fact that left our group feeling especially grateful for the privilege. Deep below the present altar are the remains of an earlier basilica built by the Roman emperor Constantine about

400CE about the time when he converted to Christianity, and ended the persecution of Christians. Deeper below the remains of the Constantinian basilica is a tomb believed to contain the bones of the Apostle Peter, who had been crucified upside down on the site and then buried there. This ancient site of Christians also had a powerful effect on our students, as one of them later noted:

> [That tour] was probably one of the most meaningful experiences of our trip. The enormous amount of faith represented there and the proof of Peter's existence were important confirmations to my own faith...I had always had the faith of other people around me, but I had simply trusted in what I believed and had been taught. Now I felt as though I had some sort of physical proof that what I believed had to be valid and it didn't matter if I was Catholic or Lutheran. We both believe in the same God, and that is what is ultimately important.

After nearly a week in Rome, we traveled far north to Wittenberg, Germany, home of the famous sites of Martin Luther, Phillip Melanchthon, and the Reformation. We saw the Castle Church and the door of the 95 Theses, viewed the tiny wooden pulpit from which Luther often preached, and visited the home the Reformer shared with his wife Katharina von Bora, their many children, and guests.

At the City Church, the group studied the Reformation altar. It shows Martin Luther as a disciple at the Last Supper with Jesus. In that same church, the students also studied a painting by Luther's contemporary Lucas Cranach theYonger, entitled "Martin Luther Tending the Vineyard of the Lord." The work emphasized the "good Lutherans" at the expense of the "bad Catholics," and stands in marked contrast to a large Catholic sculpture they had already studied while in Rome, a graphic illustration of Martin Luther and John Calvin being thrown into Hell by the triumphant figure of Religion. The sharp contrast between these two artistic renderings offered the group unmistakable illustrations of the powerful polemics each faith tradition has used in condemnation of the other through the centuries.

However, in both Rome and Wittenberg, the group also saw evidence of ways in which the historical brickbats hurled at the opposing tradition have now given way to dialogue and peaceful coexistence, even cooperation. In Rome, we met with a pastor of the German-speaking Lutheran congregation, which was established there in the 1800s, built itself a new church in 1922, and has even welcomed

Pope John Paul II to its pulpit to preach. In Wittenberg, the group met with the pastor of the sole Catholic parish of the town. Used to the demographics of the American Midwest, our students are often shocked to learn that some 85–90%of the area's population are unchurched; in the very city most identified with Reformer Martin Luther, these people are neither Catholic *nor* Lutheran, and many have never even seen the inside of a church. The enormous effort of reaching out to the unchurched, and the needy in the Wittenberg area has brought the Lutheran and Catholic churches to see in each other allies, rather than opponents. In a number of social projects, they now combine their efforts.

During our short side trip to Berlin, students were shown the results of extreme religious intolerance which shattered that country, and the entire world during the Second World War. After seeing the Peace memorial in a former church in Berlin's bustling center, the group visits the former Jewish synagogue in the much quieter Oranienberg Street. Once called the "new synagogue," the building was spared damage in the infamous Crystal Night, but then largely destroyed by firebombs later during the reign of Hitler. It has now been carefully rebuilt as a museum and Jewish cultural center for Berlin. During our visit there, our group encountered another stark reminder of intolerance and conflict in the world: the presence of high security at the usually quiet entrance to the Synagogue, including swarms of heavily armed German police using sensitive metal detectors, and conducting body searches. Sadly, its own history and the tumultuous relations between Jews and Arabs in the world today have made this Jewish center in Berlin a clear target for terrorist attack. Our students were sobered by the experience, both inside the museum and outside it.

Sadly, the Berlin Synagogue was not the first time that our students witnessed such a display of high security during our trip. There was, for many years, a New Year's Eve celebration in Rome for which there was always much anticipation. Then it abruptly stopped happening. Apparently, there had been a terrorist threat against the Pope at Christmas, and, though we were able to enjoy a lovely Vesper Service with him earlier in the evening, it seemed that no one at the Vatican was taking any chances with large public events that night. In contrast to the joyful celebration that had been held at midnight at the turn of the Millenium in 2000, St. Peter's Square was dark, cold, and almost deserted as the bells of the Basilica tolled in the New Year. A light was burning in the window of the Pope's apartment high above, but he never appeared to give his traditional greeting. Instead, at 12:05, when the last bell from the Basilica had rung, Vatican police began to force the few remaining tourists out of the square by driving their tiny cars directly at them. Over our many years of January trips abroad, it has become a memorable New Year's Eve celebration, though recently in a way hardly any of us could have anticipated.

Our last major stop on the study tour was Strasbourg, France, home of the Ecumenical Research Institute of the Lutheran World Federation. There the group met key players who helped to bring the *Joint Declaration* successfully to the signing table in Augsburg, Germany, on October 31, 1999. Primary among them was Dr. Theodor Dieter, Director of the Institute, who supported Lutheran negotiators with expert theological research throughout the long ordeal of drafting, and then the international ratification, of the document. Dieter's unwavering commitment to ecumenical understanding, his deep sorrow at difficulties and controversies raised by the *Joint Declaration*, and his tempered joy at its final passage never fails to deeply move students as they listen to his personal story.

The students were privileged to meet with a young Finnish pastor Dr. Päivi Jussila, the Assistant Study Secretary for Worship of the Lutheran World Federation in Geneva, Switzerland. Newly appointed to the LWF position in 1999, Jussila had been given the difficult task of planning all aspects of the diplomatically delicate ceremony for the historic ecumenical signing. Her work had involved many months of careful and detailed negotiation with representatives of the Vatican. Following her presentation, Jussila shared a film of the actual signing. The genuine international excitement at the historic ecumenical event in Augsburg touched our students very much and made them further appreciate how much work had gone into the passage of the document over a period of thirty years.

Before meeting the key players in Strasbourg, our students had already had a chance to experience first hand just how exacting and difficult such ecumenical work can be. After the group attended a Catholic Mass in Rome and then a Lutheran Sunday Service in Wittenberg, we asked them one afternoon in midcourse to hold a discussion on the issue of Intercommunion, that is, to pose the question, "who ought to be permitted to take communion in my church?" Each of the small groups of students had at least one ELCA member and a Roman Catholic, as well as a student from another faith tradition.

In their groups, the students found themselves pressed to articulate the tenets of their own faith traditions, often for the first time, in an encounter with another tradition. Those among them whose churches practice "closed communion" (only their own members may commune), were asked to justify the exclusion, and those whose traditions allow "open communion" (all baptized Christians are invited to commune) are equally challenged to explain that particular direction. Students were then asked to agree on some guidelines about intercommunion that might be offered to individuals and to the churches themselves. One student later reflected on the challenging experience:

> In learning about our religious differences, we must also be able to respect them, which can draw out ecumenical dialogues over a very long period. When we did the discussion about intercommunion while in Wittenberg that was really made obvious to me. We each came to the table with our own ideas of what receiving the Eucharist means and what communing together implies. Some of the group were not as willing to find a compromise because they thought the practices of their church were right, even though they were more exclusive. Others in our group had to be respectful of that person's thoughts while trying to find a solution pleasing to everyone else.... If you don't respect a person's thoughts, you risk losing their participation, which is much more powerful when it is dialogue among religious leaders, and not just college students. There are so many details and different opinions in dealing with ecumenical issues that it is no wonder it took thirty years to develop a draft of the *Joint Declaration*.

Following that unusual experience, the students talked about the significant challenge of ecumenical work for the rest of the trip, including during the concluding days in Chicago. The students were special guests of the Office for Ecumenical Affairs at the ELCA Headquarters on West Higgins Road. For two days they learned, now from an American perspective, about the drafting of the *Joint Declaration* agreement, and the other ongoing ecumenical, and interfaith dialogues, in which the ELCA is involved. They heard, as well, about the work of the ELCA's departments of Global Mission, Communications, and Higher Education and Ministry. For getting the most number of correct answers on a Global Mission quiz, one lucky student even won a free ticket to the Global Mission event for the following summer.

By the end of the three week study tour, our students had seen many significant religious sites, come to know something of the issues that have historically separated Catholics and Lutherans, studied the recent *Joint Declaration* agreement that attempts to draw them back together, and attempted ecumenical negotiation themselves. They have begun to understand what ecumenism is, and what it is not, as one student observed:

> Though I think there is a risk of conforming to others beliefs and not defending your own, that is not what ecumenism stands for. [Rather] it is to come together at common points so that we can come together as children of God. I never realized there was a problem with the issue of Justification between the Catholics and Protestants, especially in our day and age. That sort of thinking is where you find the roots of ecumenism; the place that is hard to see a divide is exactly the place to build a bridge.

With new background and understanding, some students had already begun to anticipate the hopeful directions of continued ecumenical progress. One remarked:

> Not only does the *Joint Declaration* mark a change in church relations for Lutherans and Catholics, but for other Protestant denominations as well. As one of the sheets we got at the ELCA Headquarters pointed out, Methodists, Episcopalians, and even Jews are having dialogues with Lutherans. I think it is important to realize that ecumenism doesn't just refer to Lutheran-Catholic relations, the *Joint Declaration* seems to have inspired dialogue among all Christian churches. Appropriately, this is in accord with the last point made in the *Joint Declaration* text itself, which says that the communications should be a basis for the churches to come together.

Following a small farewell dinner in Chicago, our time together ended, and the group departed for their homes and an opportunity to *try* to tell their loved ones what they had experienced on this special study tour. Despite intense contact and discussion with members of other faith traditions, no one has yet been moved to convert to another denomination. In fact, quite the opposite has occurred: many of the students voice renewed and now more conscious commitments to the traditions in which they have been raised. For a fair number, the extraordinary journey has helped them to find another new dimension too: a more mature "ownership" of their faith. The encounter with ecumenism among some of the sacred spaces of Europe has led some to a deepened understanding of their vocation to live as committed Christians in the world. One member of the group wrote:

> Spiritually, I learned so much more about my religion and what it means to be a Lutheran. To me, justification through faith defines the true Lutheran perspective...Because of visiting the sites, I now have a better understanding of being a Lutheran.

And another added:

> I will always be Catholic, and will always belong to the Catholic Church in the places I live, but I can also respect and celebrate with people of different faith traditions without questioning who is right or wrong. We all believe in the same basic truths, and as long as we can respect the differences in each other we will have ground for agreement and be doing ecumenical work on an everyday level.

The extraordinarily engaged students who traveled with us in January belong to the generation of young people that has, in the words of one speaker, "grown up with ecumenism." That they now learn in a better way what *ecumenism* means, what its challenges are, and what it may require of them and their churches can give the professors, as well as their respective colleges, reason to believe that

the future of Christian leadership is in very good hands. We commend these young people for their dedication to this crucial work.

And finally, because it tells the story so well, we conclude with one student's summary of January 2002:

> As I boarded the plane to come home from Frankfurt, Germany, I had been challenged and changed in my thinking and meaning of my life of faith. I had seen where some of the earliest Christians had been, walked in places they had, seen one of the earliest paintings of Mary holding Jesus, I had been in Rome, where Peter and Paul preached the Gospel, I had walked the steps of so many before me through Rome and Germany. Then I had gone on to see how the churches that were once together came to be divided in the distress and misunderstanding of the time. I had come to realize how Martin Luther was truly trying to reform the church and not trying to divide or go against the Pope. Starting in Germany with our discussion together on the *Doctrine of Justification* and ending in France as we heard from Theodor Dieter about his experience of negotiating the *Joint Declaration* and signing of it, I had learned and seen so much.... This was so amazing.

The overseas experiences, coupled with the intense study of the *Joint Declaration's* text, combined past, present, and future issues for a new generation that is already living ecumenically and charged with carrying out future ecumenical agreements for the churches in their lifetimes. The students returned to their respective campuses aware of some significant denominational challenges that may impede further movement toward unity among Christians, but, above all, aware in new ways of the shared history of all Christians and with renewed hope for their eventual reconciliation worldwide.

Institut für deutsche Sprache und Kultur

**Amerikaner reisen von Rom nach Wittenberg**

**Vertrag unterzeichnet - Studenten aus Minnesota kommen nun alljährlich - Katholisch-lutherischer Dialog**

**Wittenberg/MZ/mac.** Gleich drei Kurse beginnen in diesen Tagen am Institut für deutsche Sprache und Kultur in Wittenberg. An jedem nehmen junge Studenten aus den USA teil, die mehrere Tage oder aber mehrere Monate in der Lutherstadt Quartier beziehen. Für Marianne Lehker ein Zeichen dafür, dass in den Vereinigten Staaten die Existenz des Institutes mittlerweile nicht mehr unbekannt ist. Überdies spreche, so die Institutsleiterin, das Verhältnis von Qualität und Preis für Wittenberg. Wie natürlich die Geschichte der Stadt, die insbesondere Lutheraner zu einer Reise animiert.

Langjährige Verhandlungen sind mit zwei Colleges aus dem Bundesstaat Minnesota geführt worden - mit dem St. Olaf College und dem Gustavus Adolphus College. Letztlich waren sie von Erfolg gekrönt. Ein Vertrag konnte vor wenigen Wochen unterzeichnet werden.

Studenten aus Iowa üben den katholisch-lutherischen Dialog. Sie kommen aus Rom und bleiben eine Woche in Wittenberg.

Danach sollen jedes Jahr an die 25 Studenten aus Minnesota hier ein Semester absolvieren. Die ersten trafen bereits in Wittenberg ein.

Für sie ist ein so umfangreiches wie vielfältiges Programm auf die Beine gestellt worden. Neben dem Deutsch-Unterricht und den sozialen Praktika in Kindergärten oder der Wittenberger Suppenküche, neben landeskundlichen Vorträgen und einem Kunstworkshop an der Burg Giebichenstein erwarten die jungen Amerikaner drei Fachkurse an der Universität in Halle: zu Bach bis Brecht, sprich Musik- und Literaturgeschichte; zum deutschen Beitrag zur Theologie; zum Thema Deutschland und das neue Europa. Für Abwechslung sorgen Exkursionen - nach Dessau und Weimar, Leipzig und Berlin.

Aus dem Bundesstaat Wisconsin stammen acht Studenten, die am Ursprungsort der Reformation Material sammeln wollen - unter wissenschaftlichen wie touristischen Aspekten. Ziel ist die Produktion einer CD-Rom für amerikanische Hochschulen, eine Art roter Faden für künftige akademische Reisen auf den Spuren der Reformation. Keine Sprachkurse oder landeskundlichen Seminare galt es für die jungen Leute vom Carthage College vorzubereiten, das Wittenberger Institut hat sich vielmehr um die Infrastruktur gekümmert - um einen Kleinbus und um Übernachtungen bei Gastfamilien.

Schließlich ist da noch ein Reiseseminar aus Iowa. 26 Studenten zweier privater, konfessionell gebundener Hochschulen üben den „katholisch-lutherischen Dialog". Sie kommen direkt aus Rom, bleiben eine Woche in der Lutherstadt und ziehen im Anschluss nach Bayern weiter. Am Wochenende ließen sie sich durch die Altstadt führen, trafen Mitglieder der Katholischen Gemeinde. Wittenberg ist für sie indes eher eine Basisstation - für Ausflüge nach Eisleben, zur Wartburg bei Eisenach oder zur jüdischen Gemeinde nach Berlin.

*Front page article of the Wittenberg newspaper: Luther and Loras students in the town square.*

# Conclusion

**Ruth R. Kath**
Luther College

My father is blessed with the somewhat exotic sounding name of Randolph Beauregard Robert; he is a child of the deep South. My father was raised in New Orleans in a Protestant church. In 1946, he married my very Roman Catholic mother, in her native Maine. Fifty years or so ago, when a so-called "mixed marriage" such as theirs occurred between a Catholic and a Protestant, the wedding was not permitted to take place in the Catholic church itself, but rather was held quietly in the living room of the priest's house next door, in the rectory. For the wedding to take place at all, the non-Catholic spouse, in this case, my father, also had to promise—in writing—to raise any children of the union in the Catholic faith. Because my father loved my mother and did so want to marry her, he made that promise; he yielded his own church tradition for hers. Most partners in mixed marriages did that back then; it was expected of them.

*Ruth R. Kath*

It was also expected that a Protestant like my father would convert to Catholicism and abandon his own tradition completely.

Back then, before the ecumenical openness of Vatican II, people like my father were given to understand that Catholics defined the Truth, and that everyone else needed to convert to the "True Faith."—I have since learned that Protestants were similarly judgmental about their Catholic neighbors.

But my father was very attached to his own tradition and did not find this converting to be such a cut-and-dried affair. Though he tried long and hard, my father found that he could not quite accept some major parts of Catholic teachings, and so he did not convert. Nevertheless, he faithfully accompanied us to the Catholic Church every Sunday morning of my childhood. He sat in the pew with us, stood and kneeled, listened and prayed the same as we all did. But, when communion time came, he stayed behind in the seat, as the five of us kids marched like little ducks behind our mother up to the altar rail and took communion. And when we returned from our long trek to the front of the church, my father was still in his seat. He was always with us in that place, but we soon learned: he hadn't seen "the necessary light," and until he did, there could be no communion for him in that church. That was the way it was for all the years of my childhood. My father never did convert; when we five children had all grown up, he finally returned to his own Protestant tradition.

So much ecumenical healing has come since those days, and there is so much to rejoice about with the signing of the recent *Joint Declaration*. But we are reminded at the same time that there is still so much to do to bring Catholics and Protestants together in unity. Some forty years after we children left our father behind in the church pew, Catholics and Protestants do not regularly commune together. And what of all the other children of God in our world? For all its historic significance, the *Joint Declaration's* historic signing marks only the *beginning* of the work yet to do to achieve harmony and understanding among all God's people.

Some years ago, my father gave me the gift of an alb, a kind of long white baptismal gown Christians have worn for centuries. I wear it at every opportunity. Why? Because the one who was always left behind in the pew back then gave it to me as a gift—not as a sign that the tradition I grew up with is somehow set apart, or better, but rather as a sign that, though my father and I came from different church traditions, he and I—like people of faith throughout the world—can honor the differences, but above all, embrace what we share in common, as we worship the God who loves all of us. I wear my father's gift as a visible reminder that, as one ecumenical pioneer put it so beautifully, "What unites us is stronger than what separates us."

# Appendix A

The Luther College-St. John's Exchange

| Year | Luther | St. John"s |
|---|---|---|
| 1967-68 | Wilfred F. Bunge | Emeric Lawrence, O.S.B. |
| 1968-69 | Dale Johnson | Emeric Lawrence, O.S.B. |
| 1969-70 | John Sieber | Daniel Durken, O.S.B. |
| 1970-71 | Joseph Everson | Zachary Williams, O.S.B. |
| 1971-72 | Bradley Hanson | Emeric Lawrence, O.S.B. |
| 1972-73 | John Helgeland | Jerome Theisen, O.S.B., with Emeric Lawrence, O.S.B. (chaplain) |
| 1973-74 | John Helgeland | Emeric Lawrence, O.S.B. |
| 1974–75 | | Emeric Lawrence, O.S.B. (chaplain) |
| 1984 | | Emeric Lawrence, O.S.B. (chaplain) |

# Appendix B

## H. George Anderson

Dates:

1979–1990 **Co-chair U.S. Lutheran/Catholic Theological Dialogue team** finished round VII on Justification 1985

1985 *Justification by Faith: Lutherans and Catholics in Dialogue VII.* Minneapolis: Augsburg, 1985 H. George Anderson et. al., eds.

1982–1995 **President of Luther College**

1983–1991 Karen Bockelman, Campus Pastor

1991– Michael Blair, Campus Pastor

1984–1988 **Commission on Studies, Lutheran World Federation**

1986 125th anniversary of Luther College

May 5–9, 1986 Lutheran World Federation Commission meeting at Luther College focuses on theological studies, ecumenical dialogue, discussions of theological issues

1990 Initiated and finished round VIII on One Mediator: Mary and the Saints

1995–2001 **Presiding Bishop of ELCA**

1995–2001 Vice President for US: Lutheran World Federation

**1999 Signed Joint Declaration on the Doctrine of Justification as Vice President of Lutheran World Federation**

2002 Retired, returned to Luther College as Vocation Visitor

2003 Fall—taught two Luther College courses on Lutheranism

# Notes

## Footnotes

[5] Jordahl continues, "Before long such historic parishes as Paint Creek, near Waterville, Big Canoe and Washington Prairie became centers of a vital Lutheran church life. It was U.V. Koren, for more than half a century pastor at Washington Prairie, who in 1854 began conducting occasional preaching services for the few Norwegian families in Decorah. With the coming of Luther College in 1862, services became regularized with Professors Laur. Larsen and F.A. Schmidt preaching alternate Sundays in the old Winneshiek County Courthouse."

[8] While the division between Catholics and Lutherans may have started wars elsewhere, it could not compete with the Lutheran-Lutheran fireworks that erupted in Decorah. A sharp theological disagreement over the issue of salvation erupted in 1889 among the Lutherans of the town permanently changed the face of that worshipping community, when part of the congregation stayed in the old church and another marched several blocks down the street to form a separate Lutheran congregation there. The newly established congregation, located on the corner of Broadway and Winnebago streets, received the original name, Decorah Lutheran Church. The fact that [current day] First Lutheran and Decorah Lutheran churches stand only four blocks apart on the same street is a direct result of the 1889 separation...[T]he segment (a minority of the congregation) that remained with the Norwegian Synod retained use of the building and renamed itself First Lutheran Church. For the next twenty-eight years the two churches were out of fellowship with each other. Not until 1917, with a merger of the formerly contending synods, did First and Decorah become sister congregations.

[8] In his 1996 history of First Lutheran Church, Jordahl had this to say about the split, "First Lutheran Church and Decorah Lutheran were formed out of the split of the congregation originally formed in 1863. That controversy, called 'Naadevalgstriden,' was over the nature of grace and what it means when Lutherans assert salvation by grace alone. Why are some saved but not others? Is it because some, hearing the gospel, 'cooperate' with the Holy Spirit, accept the word in faith and thus are saved? Or is it because God has elected—even 'predestined'—some to come to faith?" From Jordahl, "History" in 1996 Membership Directory, First Lutheran Church

[24] Interestingly, Emeric Lawrence was Muggli 's French professor at St. John's.

[25] Following Wilfred Bunge's year at St. John's, he returned to his teaching duties at Luther College, where he taught religion and classics until his retirement in 1999.

[27] After his year at St. John's, Johnson joined the faculty of Vanderbilt Divinity School.

[28] Sieber then returned to Luther College for the rest of his career, retiring as professor emeritus in 2000.

[33] According to Barry Colman in Worship and Work, "In 1969 the Bush Foundation, St. Paul, awarded St. John's a grant of $150,000 for a continuing education program for all Minnesota clergy. The program was governed by an interdenominational board of advisors and was known as the Archibald and Edyth Bush Interdenominational Continuing Education Program for the Clergy of Minnesota. By January, 1970, twenty full scholarships for pastors and rabbis had been offered." St. John's Archives.

[35] Hanson retired as Professor emeritus in 2000. Catholic Life and Thought: A study of the Catholic Church in America in light of its historical and sociological background, its body of basic beliefs and practices, and its current situation since Vatican II. Special attention is given to comparison and contrast with Protestant positions. (Luther College Catalogue, 71.)

This wording is retained in the current catalogue.

[38] For a history of the church in Nassau, see Colman Barry's "On these Rocks: Catholics in the Bahamas. Collegeville, MN: St. John's Abbey Press, 1973.

[42] Helgeland recalled that his students at St. John's even lobbied for him to be given a tenure-track there. Helgeland, phone call with Bunge, 10 February 2002.

[45] Williams returned to St. John's the next year, but eventually left the order.

[46] Theisen later became the eighth abbot of St. John's Abbey. Interestingly, in his essay on his life as a monk of St. John's, Theisen does not make any mention of his year in Decorah.

[47] The exchange was also the direct impetus for a sizeable three-year grant given to Luther College, St. Olaf College, St. John's/St Benedict's, and St. Catherine's by the National Endowment for the Humanities (NEH). The grant focused on Christian Humanism and fostered student exchanges among the four institutions for courses based on the reader it produced, "Readings in Christian Humanism." The courses presented historical surveys of major writers of the Christian tradition through the centuries, and were offered on alternate campuses. Harris Kaasa, head of the department of Religion and Philosophy, was the Luther College representative.

[56] 1956 was the first year that seniors were not required to attend. Then, after the burning of Preus Gymnasium in November 1961, there were two chapel services daily, one for freshmen (required) and one for others (not required) in the auditorium of the sciences building. When the Field House was completed in the fall of 1964, chapel was held there, but was not required of anyone. (Will Bunge, conversation July 2004)

[97] Each of whom accepted other pastoral assignments before the first exchange actually began in the summer of 1987.

[100] In the late eighties, H. George Anderson initiated a move to strengthen another component of the college that would have a significant impact on Luther College's ecumenicity, as well. Because of Anderson's experience with worldwide ecumenical work, he wanted to increase the college's international connections. Calling for Luther's "Globalization," he authorized Professor Mark Lund of the Economic, Business, and Accounting department to establish new Luther-sponsored programs overseas and to expand other study abroad opportunities for Luther students, particularly in the January Term. Vice President for Admissions Dennis Johnson also moved to recruit a significant number of new international students, especially from the Pacific Rim and from Malta.

[101] Under the guidance of Lutheran co-chair Paul Empie, Round VII of the Lutheran-Catholic Dialogue on the issue of Justification had begun in 1978, but Empie died suddenly one year later.

[102] Lehmann, Karl and Wolfhart Pannenberg, eds. Lehrverurteilungen—kirchentrennend? Freiburg im Breisgau: Herder, 1988 and Göttingen: Vandenhoeck & Ruprecht, 1988. Published in English translation as: The Condemnations of the Reformation Era: Do They Still Divide? Minneapolis: Fortress, 1990.

[109] In October 1994, the Center for Faith and Life stage had hosted quite a different kind of ecumenical event: The newly appointed Archbishop Jerome Hanus, O.S.B. was formally welcomed to the area of northeast Iowa, part of the archdiocese of Dubuque. (Note: Coadjutor Archbishop since August 1994, he succeeded to the See in October 1995.) The CFL on the Luther College campus offered the only place large enough for all to gather who attended the formal ceremony, including representatives of the college and several of the Protestant churches in the area. Luther College Campus Pastor, Norene A. Smith, brought the greeting on behalf of Luther College. The well-attended event served to further solidify ecumenical connections with the Dubuque archdiocese and among all the churches of the area.

[117] Kasper is now the President.

# Endnotes

## Introduction

[1] *For a list of exchangees see appendix A.*

[2] Bunge, Wilfred F. Luther College: Who We Are. (pamphlet for orientation of Luther faculty and staff) Luther College, 2002.

[3] Luther College Mission Statement. Luther College Catalogue. 2003–5.

[4] Jordahl, Leigh. "125 Years at First Lutheran" in Pictorial Directory of First Lutheran Church, Decorah, Iowa, 1989.

[6] Hoffmann, Rev. M. M. Centennial History of the Archdiocese of Dubuque 1837–1937. Dubuque, Iowa: Columbia College Press, 1938, 119.

[7] Ibid.

[9] Bunge, Wilfred F. e-mail to author, 23 June 2002.

[10] Jordahl, Leigh D. and Harris F. Kaasa. Stability and Change: Luther College In Its Second Century. Decorah, Iowa: The Luther College Press, 1986, 70–1.

[11] Joint Declaration on the Doctrine of Justification, ¶ 4.

## Chapter 1

[12] Farwell, E.D. letter to Fr. Emeric Lawrence, 17 May 1974, Luther College Archives, file 018969 Lawrence.

[13] Luther College Catalogue, 2003–5, 14.

[14] Bunge, Wilfred F. "Father Emeric Lawrence, O.S.B.: Eighty-five Years," Agora, Vol. 6. #1, Fall 1993, 4.

[15] Farwell, E. D. telephone conversation with author, 20 March 2002.

[16] Jordahl, Leigh D. and Harris F. Kaasa. Stability and Change: Luther College In Its Second Century. Decorah, Iowa: The Luther College Press, 1986, 70.

[17] Farwell, E.D. Letter to Father Emeric Lawrence, 17 May 1974, Luther College Archives, file 018969 Lawrence.

[18] Bunge, Wilfred F. "Father Emeric Lawrence, O.S.B.: Eighty-five Years." 4.

[19] E. D. Farwell, telephone conversation with author, 20 March 2002.

[20] Bunge, Wilfred F. "Father Emeric Lawrence, O.S.B.: Eighty-five Years." 4.

[21] Ibid.

[22] Bunge, Wilfred F. Farewell memo, May 26, 1975 St. John's Archives.

[23] Byrne, James. letter to Colman Barry, 28 February 1967 in St. John's Archives.

[26] Bunge, Wilfred F. St. John's, 11.

[29] Sieber. e-mail to author, 9 November 2002.

[30] Ibid.

[31] Ibid.

[32] Everson. e-mail to author, 3 December 2002.

[34] Everson. e-mail to Wilfred F. Bunge, 17 October 2002.

[36] St. John's Archives, 1971–72 catalogue.

[39] Everson. e-mail to author, 4 December 2002.

[40] Ibid.

[41] Ibid.

[43] Durken, Daniel, O.S.B. A Sense of Place II: The Benedictines of Collegeville. Collegeville, Minnesota: The Liturgical Press, 1990, 66–7.

[44] Durken. e-mail to author, 20 August 2001.

[48] Lawrence, Emeric Anthony. 1908–1999. Papers, 1932–1992. SJA Manuscript Collection 15. St. John's Abbey. Collegeville, Minnesota. 12 December 1974.

Chapter 2

[49] Lawrence, Fr. Emeric. unpublished manuscript, The Lutheran Journals of a Catholic Monk. 17, 19.

[50] Bunge, Wilfred F. "Father Emeric Lawrence, O.S.B.: Eighty-five Years." 5.

[51] Ibid., 4.

[52] Lawrence. Journals, 7.

[53] Ibid., 85.

[54] Ibid., 16.

[55] Ibid., 10.

[57] Ibid., 60–1.

[58] Ibid.

[59] Lawrence, Emeric A. "A Monk at Luther," St. John's 8, no. 2 (Summer 1968): 16.

[60] Lawrence. Journals, 67.

[61] Lawrence, Emeric A. "A Monk at Luther." 14.

[62] Ibid.

[63] Ibid.

[64] Ibid. , 53.

[65] Lawrence, Emeric A. "A Monk at Luther." 16.

[66] Lawrence. Journals, 94.

[67] Ibid., 73.

[68] Wrightsman, Bruce. St John's 16, no. 1 (Summer 1975): 15.

[69] Lawrence. Journals, 73.

[70] Ibid., 83.

[71] Ibid. , 11–2.

[72] Ibid., 251.

[73] Ibid., 81.

[74] Ibid.

[75] Epistle 9, March 25, 1974.

[76] Bunge, Wilfred F. "Father Emeric Lawrence, O.S.B.: Eighty-five Years." 6.

[77] Lawrence. Journals, 105.

[78] Ibid., 160.

[79] Ibid., 66.

[80] Ibid.

[81] Ibid., 81.

[82] Ibid.

[83] Ibid., 67.

[84] Ibid.

[85] Ibid., 73.

[86] Ibid., 77.

[87] Ibid., 85.

[88] Ibid., 179.

[89] Decorah Journal. 15 June 1975. Photograph clipping with caption, in Luther College Archives.

[90] Decorah Journal

. 8 May 1974. Photograph clipping with caption, in Luther College Archives.

[91] Lawrence. Journals, 262.

[92] Ibid., 4.

[93] Ibid., 82.

[94] St. John's, 15.

[95] Lawrence. Journals, letter July 1967, 5–6.

[96] Lawrence. Journals, 245–7.

**Chapter 3**

[98] For a chronology of President Anderson's career see appendix B.

[99] Lutheran-Roman Catholic Service of the Word, Augsburg Press, 1986, #12–1581

[103] Anderson, G. and J. Francis Stafford and Joseph A. Burgess, eds. The One Mediator, the Saints, and Mary. Lutherans and Catholics in Dialogue VIII, Minneapolis: Augsburg, 1992.

[104] Anderson, H. George. letter to Stafford, 25 April 1990, Luther archives.

[105] Dulles. letter to H. George Anderson, 7 May 1990, Luther archives.

[106] Stafford. letter to H. George Anderson, 10 May 1990, Luther archives.

[107] Reumann. letter to H. George Anderson, 8 May 1990, Luther archives.

[108] Gros, Jeffrey. Harvesting unpublished manuscript, 1992, 8.

[110] #8 Thesis ELCA News Release from 1997 Churchwide Assembly, Online, 19 August 1997.

[111] #13 Thesis H. George Anderson conversation with author, 14 October 1997, and ELCA News Release, 19 August 1997.

[112] #11 Thesis ELCA News Release, August 19, 1997.

[113] Justification By Faith Through Grace: Study Resources for Congregations and Parishes. Canadian Conference of Catholic Bishops and the Evangelical Lutheran Church in Canada, Ottowa, 1999, 5–6.

[114] "Lutherans and Catholics have Bridged Theological Divide"

Lutheran World Information, 23 October 1999.

[115] Koenig, Richard E. "Ecumenical Impasse?: The Vatican on Justification by Faith, The Christian Century, 14 October 1998: 926.

[116] Anderson, H. George. conversation with author, 10 July 1998.

[118] Agora, Spring 1999, 26.

[119] Justification by Faith Through Grace, 11.